Healing
Feelings...

From Your Heart

Karol K. Truman

Books by Karol K. Truman

Looking Good, Feeling Great
Feelings Buried Alive Never Die . . .

Healing

Feelings...

From Your Heart

First Printing, 2000
Second Printing, 2001

KAROL KUHN TRUMAN

Healing Feelings . . . From Your Heart
Copyright © 2000 Olympus Distributing
Cover painting, design and flip book: Valerieann J. Skinner
Editor: Donald C. Hoefelmann

Published by Olympus Distributing
P.O. Box 97693, Las Vegas, Nevada 89193-7693
All rights reserved. Printed in the U.S.A.
No part of this book may be reproduced or transmitted in any form
or by any means, electronic or mechanical, including photocopying,
recording, or by any information storage and retrieval system,
without permission in writing from the publisher.

Truman, Karol Kuhn–
Looking Good Feeling Great
Feelings Buried Alive Never Die . . .
Healing Feelings . . . From Your Heart
1. Self-Help 2. Emotional Healing 3. Forgiveness 4. Love
5. Self-Discovery 6. Personal Growth 7. Mind/Body Healing
8. Self-Healing 9. Spiritual Healing 10. Spiritual Awakening

Library of Congress Catalog Card Number: 00 090457

ISBN: 0-911207-04-X $14.95

Dedication

To God the Father and the Son,

whose love for each of us is

unfathomable and immeasurable!

And to each of you, my sisters and brothers,

who are striving for a better understanding

of that love—bringing it into your life—

and making it an enduring part of your Be-ing.

And . . .

To one of my greatest teachers, my dear

departed Mother,

who left the earth while this book was being completed.

To her goes my deepest love and gratitude for her

unending love, acceptance and support of me and my

purpose.

Contents

Acknowledgments

How does one begin to adequately acknowledge all the people who were instrumental in bringing this book to fruition? There are **so** many who made a difference.

To my dear Mother and Father, who gave me the opportunity of life and learning, and the courage to change and grow. They are together now in a better place.

To my husband, who continues to teach me and be a balancer in my life. His love and support in all I do has been unending, for which I will be forever grateful.

To our children and their spouses, for their support and patience! To them goes my eternal gratitude and love for the teachers they are and continue to be.

To Valerieann Skinner, whose patience goes beyond that of Job's. Without her this book may never have been. It has evolved through more than one title, three cover paintings and several designs, during which she was infinitely flexible. My appreciation for her diligence is more than I can adequately express.

To Anne Surowski and Frank X. Harris, who assisted me in seeing through the eyes of the abused—to the extent that I could without having been there. Their courage and tenacity in healing their wounds and scars deserves a medal. My appreciation for their added insight is immeasurable.

To Randall and Marla Vaughan, who were willing to read the first draft of the book and give me vital suggestions. Their support, encouragement, and caring is invaluable to me.

To Joyce Davis, who has always been there as a sounding board and caring advisor, even before *Feelings Buried Alive Never Die* . . . . She never ceases to have brilliant and meaningful input. My gratitude to her is unending.

To Nancy Peterson for her significant contribution; for being there to "bounce things off of." Her insight, understanding, and support is timely and truly appreciated.

To the many friends who are unmentioned, for what you have taught me, for your input, support, and caring. Your contribution has been priceless, and I feel honored to have you in my life.

To Annette Gomm for getting me started on re-editing this book. I appreciate and thank her for her valuable input.

To the countless people with whom I have worked and the readers of *Feelings Buried Alive Never Die.* . . who have shared with me by letter, phone, fax, and e-mail. You have truly taught me, blessed my life, and fostered my understanding. You have shown me how powerful and indomitable the human spirit is!

And most importantly, to the Creator of us all . . . for His unending love and patience as we continue striving to "get it"; for allowing each one of us our singular journey without interfering in our learning process; and for providing unseen assistance when we are not able to do it on our own. My deepest gratitude to Him for sustaining us with angels in disguise, those friends, acquaintances and strangers who help us move through our challenges in life. How Great Thou Art!

Preface

Several years ago a few people suggested to me that I would write another book. My reaction was, "Oh, please don't say that. Two is enough." And I quickly dismissed the suggestion, hoping it wasn't true. Three years had gone into the creation of my last book, *Feelings Buried Alive Never Die . . .* , and those years were pretty intense. It was nice not having something continually waiting for completion. I liked being free from the constant pressure of getting to the computer and finishing a book.

Then in 1996 I was revising "The Feelings Journey," a set of six companion tapes for *Feelings Buried Alive,* and as I recorded tape number four, something happened. Right in the middle of speaking the dialogue, I heard, "This is the basis for your next book." Even though I was talking at the time, I couldn't deny what I had heard. I had been given direction—loud and clear. My reaction was, "Oh. That'll be a piece of cake. I can handle this assignment," because most of it (I thought) was already done. And because it seemed so simple, I presumed the book could be put together very quickly. How wrong I was! The material on the tape, I discovered, was just the skeleton for the book. What I thought would take me months has taken me years.

Writing a book is like having a full-time job, with a lot of overtime! Except that when there are other matters to tend to (of which there are many daily), the book gets put on hold—often. My daughter finally asked me, "Mom, are you ever going to finish that book?" My reply was, "Honey, if I could have two weeks of uninterrupted time, it would get finished!" Well, those two weeks never materialized, but the book is finished at last. I think it had to be completed in God's time, not Karol's. There are many things that never would have been put into the book if I had completed it according to my own agenda.

Now that the muscles, tendons, blood, and flesh have been added to the skeleton, I recognize that *Healing Feelings . . . From Your Heart* conveys what I have come to understand on my journey. It is a narrative of the things with which I have struggled and come to grips. Sharing with others these experiences and the principles and understanding I have gained from them has been very gratifying. Many are savoring the benefits of applying these same principles, and their load has been lightened.

My basic premise is: We are all in this learning experience of life together. We are *all* God's children looking for answers. All of you are very precious in God's eyes—and mine. He taught me many years ago to see His children through His eyes, not mine. Admittedly, sometimes this is a challenge; but if I stray the course, He has His way of bringing me back.

If you have found answers that you would like to share with me, I would be happy to receive them. Likewise, I trust you will gain something of worth from this book, because you and I are more alike than we are different. Each one of us is as important as the other. And wherever we are on our life's journey it is all right. Perhaps these pages will resonate with you and assist you in understanding to a greater degree the value of discovering who you really are— the Truth of your *Be-ing*.

Please understand that the purpose of this book is to share and perhaps stimulate your thinking. Know that no matter where you are on your path, it's perfect. Know that if you desire improving your life circumstances, that is entirely possible, and perfect too.

Prologue

Have you ever ached emotionally? Have you ever experienced non-physical pain somewhere inside but were unable to pinpoint the exact spot that hurt? How would you best describe the ache? Was it a feeling of total aloneness or emptiness? Was it a feeling of abandonment—like there was no one there for you? Maybe the emotional ache resembled a deep void; and no matter how you endeavored, it could not be filled. Did you feel unworthy? Or perhaps the feeling was of deep sorrow or grief—even despair. Do any of these feelings resonate with you?

Have you ever felt that you didn't matter, that you were completely insignificant and no one would even miss you if you weren't here? Or, have you had the feeling that everything was hopeless—that there were no answers to what was happening in your life, no hope for change? Did you ever feel that your feelings were not important to anyone, and that no one really cared anyway? Whatever it was, did you feel totally helpless in your ability to remedy that ache—big or little?

If you aren't identifying in any way with the above text, is it possible that your feelings have been completely turned off? Maybe it hurts too much to feel, and you are functioning purely in a survival mode. Or without realizing it, could it be that due to a fear of "feeling" your feelings, you have literally disconnected from your *Self*?

Have you ever actually taken the opportunity to "go within" and become acquainted with your feelings—the feelings that govern existence, the feelings waiting to be acknowledged and identified, and the feelings that lead you to knowing your True Self?

There may be those of you who have your life together to such an extent that for you it's just a case of "mind over matter." You may have the ability to set your intent to "re-forming" whatever needs re-forming. I anticipate, however, that many of you do identify with what I am saying. You've been there, done that, and would like additional insight because you don't care to be there or do that again.

If you are searching for answers that will assist you or someone else in alleviating any ache still inside, perhaps this book will provide some understanding and help you find solutions for opening the door—to *Healing Feelings . . . From Your Heart.*

Food For Thought
That which is in your heart is what you take with you.

Where do our feelings reside? In our head or in our heart? Don't we think with our head and feel with our heart?

Why do we use the expressions: "My heart aches for you." "I thought my heart would break." "My heart went out to her." "Listen with your heart." "It tears my heart in two." "You're breaking my heart." "What a heart-wrenching experience!" "My heart cries for them." "They just lost heart and quit." "My heart was filled to overflowing," and so on? Isn't it interesting how many expressions we use referencing our heart?

When we are humiliated by someone, does that hurt our head or our heart? When we are wrongfully accused of something, does that affect our head or our heart? When one or both of our parents show disapproval of us, does that hurt our head or our heart? When we feel worthless or unlovable, where does *that* feeling register?

If a loved one dies, do our feelings of grief and loss affect our head or our heart? When we truly love someone, is that feeling in our head or our heart? When we hear about something tragic happening in a family or listen to a person tell a *heartbreaking* story that causes us to get teary-eyed, are those feelings coming from our head or our heart?

Yes, we *feel* that person's pain, or our own pain, with our heart.

On a daily basis, in our normal walk of life, do we see more people "coming from" their head or their heart? Now my final question: Where do you "come from"? Where do you choose coming from—your head or your heart?

Note: In the text there are many words hyphenated that aren't normally hyphenated. I do this deliberately for the purpose of drawing attention to the context of the word. It is a way of seeing the words through different eyes, e.g. *Re-claim*—the point being that something was ours at one time; perhaps we lost it or let it go unknowingly. But, we couldn't be *re-claiming* it if it hadn't already been ours in the first place. *Re-connect* is another one. Here again, we were at one time connected or we couldn't *re-connect*. When you notice these words, my hope is that you will "see" them through different eyes, and in a new, and perhaps more meaningful, way . . . keeping that focus throughout the book.

Introduction

THE SCRIPT

In this exciting, magnificent, electro-magnetic universe of ours, everything found in, on, under and above it has unique vibrational frequencies! Literally everything is an energy vibration. This includes our feelings and our thoughts.

Physicists tell us that a thought has an independent force all its own and that it can produce effects which form a field, called a thought-field. The energy of a feeling also produces a field. Like everything else, these energy fields have vibrational frequencies and can be changed. Consequently, it is possible to change the vibrations of feelings and thoughts that we consider negative into ones that are positive.

Now, although our true, unadulterated essence is one of pure Love, it is impacted here on earth by the energies around us. When we experience the negative, including the negative in our own feelings and thoughts, it can slowly obscure the truth of who we are. As negativity mounts in our *Be-ing*, little by little the memory of perfection in our DNA becomes veiled and clouded. Eventually, the negativity may create a false self that masks our true self, the Love that we are.

In this book, *Healing Feelings . . . From Your Heart*, of the multiplicity of energies that impact each of us on a daily basis, we are concerned with the energies of our feelings, thoughts, words, and behavior; how they impact our state of Be-ing; and how their negative effects can be recognized, processed, and resolved.

One of the several "tools" available for resolving our negative feelings is the *Script*, and you will find references to it and to *Scripting* throughout the book. The *Script* will be familiar to those of you who have read *Feelings Buried Alive Never Die. . . .* The term "Scripting" was coined by readers of the *Feelings . . .* book and by attendees of my seminars who had utilized the *Script* on a consistent basis. It means "using the *Script*." For those of you new to this concept, allow me to provide a brief overview and acquaint you with the *Script* at this time.

There is a facet of our *Be-ing* that remembers and knows everything about us there is to know. This part of us has forgotten nothing. Some call this facet of our *Be-ing*, Intelligence. Others call it Higher Self. We may also refer to it as Super Conscious or as Spirit. I choose calling it *Spirit*. Now, when I say Spirit, I am referring to *my* Spirit—no one else's. And should you use the term Spirit to refer to the all-knowing facet of *Self*, then you will be referring to *your* Spirit—that part of your Soul remembering everything about you—no one else. So, it's our own Spirit we access when we use the *Script*.

Our *Be-ing* (Soul) is comprised of Spirit and Body. Having been schooled by our senses from birth, our human nature is to listen to the needs and the wants of our bodies. So naturally, the desires of the body seem to receive the most attention, thereby governing our actions and existence. Because of this, our Spirit is often neglected—much to the detriment of both Body *and* Spirit. If we desire to function as a whole—a whole Be-ing—and to be at peace in both Body and Spirit (in our Soul), then the body cannot be in charge or be allowed to overrule our Spirit. Both need to be balanced, to be in harmony.

Because most of us have allowed our body to "call the shots," we have experienced inner conflict and frustration. Because I had allowed my body to be the master, I found that life was not bringing me the peace and joy I knew was possible. When I finally acknowledged this, I decided to do something about it. Upon discovering the *Script*, I realized I had found a precious gem that could possibly help me eliminate my inner conflicts. But first it was necessary for me to become aware, conscious, and mindful of my feelings, thoughts, and words so that I could correct the disharmony—the conflict that was going on between my Body and my Spirit—causing fragmentation in my Soul.

Whenever I recognized a thought or feeling that was creating *dis-harmony* I went through the *Script* stating that thought or feeling. I then gave my Spirit instructions to correct the erroneous programming that was the cause of my discomfort. The results were remarkable!

Dr. Deepak Chopra, MD indicates in his books that the cells' memory of perfection, which is contained in the DNA, cannot be lost. It can only be covered over, at which point the perfect blueprint of the cell is distorted. It is distorted by incorrect perceptions and erroneous programming, which alter the perfect blueprint and, in turn, distort the cells. Use of the *Script* reverses this erroneous programming.

When I address my Spirit as I use the *Script*, I am talking to and instructing no one except *my* Higher Self, *my*

Intelligence, *my* Spirit. Upon my addressing it, my Spirit goes to the negative feeling that has covered the memory of perfection in my DNA, knocks on the door, and tells the feeling that answers the door that she (my Spirit) has been requested by her Body to make some corrections. In other words, she has been requested to clean house, to uncover the memory of perfection contained in the cells' original perfect blueprint, and to eliminate the distortion. This is done by *re-programming* to restore the cells' perfect function and bring harmony and balance back to my DNA.

As I do this, I become responsible for myself and *account-able* for what I think and feel. I am facilitating my own "shift," my own transformation, by uncovering the memory of perfection in the cells throughout my body. The cells can then begin functioning as they were designed to function. The cells can realign themselves to become balanced and more in tune with Universal Laws—with God's Laws. Note: should you prefer using the term *Divine Intelligence, Super-Conscious,* or *Higher Self* instead of *Spirit* in addressing the all-knowing facet of yourself, the same principles apply and the *Script* still works effectively. Please, do not allow any words contained within the *Script* to trigger discomfort in you. Feel free to modify any terminology that makes using the *Script* more compatible with your beliefs.

Processing With the Script

Spirit/Super-Conscious/Intelligence or Higher Self (whichever you choose), please locate the origin of my feeling(s)/thought(s) of _____. Take each and every level, layer, area, and aspect of my Be-ing to this origin. Analyze and resolve it perfectly with God's truth.

Come forward in time, healing every incident based upon the origin, according to God's will, until I'm at the present, filled with "light and truth," "God's peace and love," forgiveness of myself for my incorrect perceptions, forgiveness of every person, place, circumstance, and event contributing to this feeling/thought.

With total forgiveness and unconditional love I delete the old from my DNA, release it, and let it go now! I feel _____ (Replace old negative feeling(s)/thought(s) w/appropriate positive feeling(s)/thought(s).)

I allow every physical, mental, emotional, and spiritual problem, and inappropriate behavior based on the old feeling(s) to quickly disappear.

(Note: It isn't necessary, but I also like adding the following last sentences. And being Christian, I like doing the whole *Script* in the name of Jesus Christ, even though it isn't a prayer.)

Thank you, Spirit, for coming to my aid and helping me attain the full measure of my creation. Thank you, thank you, thank you! I love you and praise God from whom all blessings flow.

The question has been asked, "Does the *Script* take the place of prayer?" The answer to this question is an emphatic NO! The Script is not a prayer. With the Script you are addressing your Spirit, Higher Self, Intelligence (or whatever fits your belief system). In so doing you are directing your conscious thoughts and words rather than allowing unconscious, undirected, mindless thoughts and words to create your reality. When using the Script, your intent is to take responsibility for your "less than glorious" thoughts and feelings. Think of it as a tool to re-program any distorted cells brought about by negativity. The Script is a vehicle of transformational healing for all facets of your life.

This is different from praying. When praying you are talking to God, not to your own higher intelligence. And in so doing, you are directing your thoughts and words to your Heavenly Father, or Deity as you define Him/Her. In my mind, one cannot compare the two. It may seem strange to some to be conversing with their Spirit or to be giving it instructions. Most of us are not taught to do this, so it is quite a change—one that some may not wish to make. However, we carry on conversations and talk to ourselves all of the time. Ask yourself: Who is it inside my head that I am talking to, anyway?

If giving instructions to your Spirit takes you out of your comfort zone (as it did me, at first), then you may find *Healing Feelings . . . From Your Heart* a challenge. Nevertheless, be willing to step out of your comfort zone and experience some discomfort; that is when real growth takes place! Be willing to acknowledge that you may, indeed, have some incorrect perceptions. Be willing to stretch. Be willing to shift into a higher gear!

The marvelous and rewarding by-product of improving ourselves is that those around us begin improving also. It has been said that when we lift ourselves, we lift 30,000 other people with us. Even if we were to lift only one-tenth of 30,000, any amount of discomfort would be worth the effort.

Other questions which have been asked about the Script are: "Isn't the Script just a band-aid?" "How do we come to understand what we are supposed to be learning if the Script resolves our feelings without pain?"

God's ways are simple. The Script is simple. We humans are the ones who have complicated things. Some of us believe things have to be hard or that we have to suffer before we can move on. This isn't necessarily true. Nor do we always need to go back into the past and dredge up all the "old stuff." Heretofore, this is what we've known to do, and it's still fine to do it. Going back into the old stuff is sometimes necessary for our peace of mind or for knowing what is blocking our emotional progress in life. The one thing we need to guard against, however, is continuing to give energy or power to the old stuff, or getting stuck in it by constantly rehearsing the past. Somewhere along the way we need to stop clinging to it.

Sooner or later—at the perfect time for you—*Scripting* will automatically bring up whatever is imperative for you to have a conscious knowledge of. You will know when that time comes. In the meantime, you can do a lot on your own by taking the responsibility of dealing with your everyday undesirable feelings. You will still learn what you need to learn. Sometimes during this process you may even feel a need to go to a therapist or counselor who can help you move through something that you may be "stuck" on. This is perfect too. Perhaps eventually you will not even need the Script or other tools because you will be able to immediately access your "inner knowing" and go right to the cause of what is taking you out of harmony. This is the ultimate goal.

Countless readers of *Feelings Buried Alive Never Die . . .* have shared by phone, fax, or letter the impact of the Script in their lives and how it has so remarkably changed their undesirable feelings. I have personally witnessed its power in the lives of thousands of others as well, many of whom have attended my seminars or worked with me individually.

Just know that there is not a word powerful enough to describe how this method of changing my feelings and thoughts, and subsequently my life, has benefitted me and my family. Living my life so that the Savior's life, as it concerns me, will not have been in vain, continues to be the greatest desire of my heart.

Let me also say that the Script is not "mine." I am only the author of the book, not the author of the Script. The Script came through Heavenly direction after much prayer. This tool (along with others contained in this book) for purifying your heart—for *Healing Feelings . . . From Your Heart*—has the capacity to make a significant contribution to your life, should you desire it.

Please realize that there are many "roads to Rome." I am not suggesting that the several tools in this book are the only avenues for arriving there. On the contrary, I am very quick to embrace any true principle that may assist a person on their journey. I continually encourage people to read books and to attend seminars or workshops that will help them gain a greater understanding of who they really are— of their True and Divine Self.

My hope is that all of us find the tools we need for discovering our Truth, and that we use them and internalize them! Let us be more than observers. Let us participate, for it is by participating that we experience a difference and come to discover and know our *Self.* My sincere prayer is that God will be with each of us in this endeavor of self-discovery and that we will, indeed, experience **healing feelings** from our heart!

CHAPTER 1

What Happened?

*"I must do something," will always solve more problems than,
"Something must be done."*

—Unknown

The following was recently forwarded to me by a friend via e-mail. The message struck such a deep chord in my soul that I knew it had a definite place in this manuscript.

On Thursday, May 27, 1999, Darrell Scott, the father of Rachel Scott, a victim of the Columbine High School shootings in Littleton, Colorado, was invited to address the House Judiciary Committee's sub-committee. What he said to our national leaders during this special session of Congress was painfully truthful. It needs to be heard by every parent, every teacher, every politician, every sociologist, every psychologist, and every so-called expert!

These courageous words spoken by Darrell Scott are powerful, penetrating, and deeply personal. There is no doubt that God sent this man as a voice crying in the wilderness. The following is a portion of the transcript:

Since the dawn of creation there has been both good and

evil in the heart of men and women. We all contain the seeds of kindness or the seeds of violence. The death of my wonderful daughter, Rachel Joy Scott, and the deaths of that heroic teacher and the other eleven children who died must not be in vain. Their blood cries out for answers.

The first recorded act of violence was when Cain slew his brother Abel out in the field. The villain was not the club he used. Neither was it the National "Club" Association. The true killer was Cain, and the reason for the murder could only be found in Cain's heart.

In the days that followed the Columbine tragedy, I was amazed at how quickly fingers began to be pointed at groups such as the National Rifle Association. I am not a member of the NRA. I am not a hunter. I do not even own a gun. I am not here to represent or defend the NRA because I don't believe that they are responsible for my daughter's death. Therefore I do not believe that they need to be defended. If I believed they had anything to do with Rachel's murder I would be their strongest opponent. I am here today to declare that Columbine was not just a tragedy—it was a spiritual event that should be forcing us to look at where the real blame lies! Much of the blame lies here in this room. Much of the blame lies behind the pointing fingers of the accusers themselves. I wrote a poem just four nights ago that expresses my feelings best. This was written way before I knew I would be speaking here today.

> Your laws ignore our deepest needs
> Your words are empty air
> You've stripped away our heritage
> You've outlawed simple prayer
> Now gunshots fill our classrooms

> And precious children die
> You seek for answers everywhere
> And ask the question "Why?"
> You regulate restrictive laws
> Through legislative creed
> And yet you fail to understand
> That God is what we need!

Men and woman are three-part beings. We all consist of body, soul, and spirit. When we refuse to acknowledge a third part of our make-up, we create a void that allows evil, prejudice, and hatred to rush in and wreak havoc.

Spiritual influences were present within our educational systems for most of our nation's history. Many of our major colleges began as theological seminaries. This is a historical fact.

What has happened to us as a nation? We have refused to honor God, and in doing so, we open the doors to hatred and violence. And when something as terrible as Columbine's tragedy occurs, politicians immediately look for a scapegoat such as the NRA. They immediately seek to pass more restrictive laws that continue to erode away our personal and private liberties.

We do not need more restrictive laws. Eric and Dylan would not have been stopped by metal detectors. No amount of gun laws can stop someone who spends months planning this type of massacre.

The real villain lies within our own hearts. Political posturing and restrictive legislation are not the answers. The young people of our nation hold the key. There is a spiritual awakening taking place that will not be squelched! We do not need more religion. We do not need more gaudy television evangelists spewing out verbal religious garbage. We do not need more million dollar church buildings built while people with basic needs are being ignored. We do need a change of heart and a humble acknowledgment that this nation was founded on the principle of simple trust in God! As my son Craig lay under that table in the school library and saw his two friends murdered before his very eyes, he did not hesitate to pray in school. I defy any law or politician to deny him that right! I challenge every young person in America, and around the world, to realize that on April 20, 1999, at Columbine High School—prayer was brought back to our schools.

Do not let the many prayers offered by those students be in vain. Dare to move into the new millennium with a sacred disregard for legislation that violates your God–given right to communicate with Him.

To those of you who would point your finger at the NRA, I give to you a sincere challenge. Dare to examine your own heart before casting the first stone!

My daughter's death will not be in vain. The young people of this country will not allow that to happen!

After reading this message, my mind flooded with many questions: Is there anything we can do to help change this whole scenario? Is there anything each of us can genuinely contribute that could bring about a re-storing—that could turn us from blaming to looking inside our own hearts and taking responsibility for our own actions? How can we bring about more love, humility, and compassion as well as more tenderness, understanding, and acceptance?

If we were able to re-store these qualities, would it help in repairing and improving the social and emotional climate of our families, our communities, our country, and our world? What is keeping us from making this change?

Could this much needed restoration conceivably be a return to our hearts, a *looking* and *seeing* through our hearts, rather than through our color-blind eyes? How can we learn to *listen* and *hear* with our hearts, rather than with our deaf ears?

Would any of us benefit by defusing our emotional time bombs, by healing the detrimental feelings we hold in our hearts—our emotional hearts? Could anyone you know benefit by healing feelings from their heart? What would this world be like if the majority of humankind exhibited more caring, honor, respect, understanding, and good will?

Just how does one bring about this healing?

Let me pick up where I left off in my book, *Feelings Buried Alive Never Die* . . . and quote something I have always cherished:

PRAYER BY ST. FRANCIS OF ASSISI

Lord, make me an instrument of Thy peace.
Where there is hatred, let me sow love.
Where there is injury, pardon.
Where there is doubt, faith.
Where there is despair, hope.
Where there is darkness, light.
Where there is sadness, joy.

Oh, Divine Master, grant that I may not so much seek,
To be consoled, as to console,
To be understood, as to understand,
To be loved, as to love.
For it is in giving, that we receive.
It is in pardoning, that we are pardoned.

It is in dying [the false self], that we are born
To Eternal Life.

For many years after first reading this prayer, I felt a great desire for being an instrument of peace and an emissary for people who are experiencing the injury and doubt, the darkness and despair spoken of in the prayer. And where St. Francis says:

Oh, Divine Master,
grant that I may not so much seek,
To be consoled, as to console,
To be understood, as to understand.
To be loved, as to love . . . ,

I came to realize how truly vital it is for each of us, in healing the injury and the doubt, the darkness and the sadness, to first be concerned with consoling the other person instead of needing to be consoled ourselves; to first sincerely strive for understanding of the other person rather than expecting them to understand us; and to first love the other person *and* our *Self* before expecting them to love us. For if we don't love our *Self*, how can we expect others to love us?

While writing out the "Prayer by St. Francis of Assisi" for the last time before going to press with *Feelings Buried Alive*, tears began streaming down my face as I *finally* started grasping the real message. In asking to be an instrument of God's peace, when it says, "Where there is hatred, let me sow love," it doesn't mean where there is hatred out there. It means, where there is hatred toward others *inside my own heart*—let me sow love. And it doesn't mean where there is injury out there. It means, where there is injury inside my heart—let me sow pardon. Nor does it mean where there is doubt out there, or despair out there, or darkness or sadness out there. No! All of a sudden I understood the true meaning of this prayer! This prayer means that where all these feelings are inside me—*inside my heart*—let me sow love, replacing hatred; let me sow pardon, replacing injury; faith, replacing doubt; hope, replacing despair; light, replacing darkness; and joy, replacing sadness, all *within my own heart!*

What exhilaration filled my soul when I realized this! How could I have been so far off base, thinking the prayer always meant out there? Why hadn't I seen this before? Did everyone else get it but me? Of course, the answer is, It doesn't matter. Just as long as you finally get it.

Is it possible St. Francis of Assisi realized that through the process of life people lose touch with their True Self? He must have known the qualities with which we came, and the importance of re-storing or re-turning to them.

How and where do we begin replacing hatred, replacing injury, replacing doubt, despair, darkness and sadness? How do we begin *Healing Feelings . . . From Our Heart?* Before we can answer this question, it is essential to understand the process of our emotional growth from the time of conception forward—what we were when we came here and how our life's journey contributes to the Be-ing we become.

Jon R.G. Turner, founder of Whole-Self Psychology, suggests that along with our genetic coding (DNA) we inherit mother and father's emotional states during conception, and the nine months prior to birth. Yes, the foundation upon which each life is set is determined by how Mom and Dad feel about themselves and about each other at the time of conception. Their feelings, thoughts, and attitudes constitute the basis of our emotional DNA. These patterns are then activated after birth. See Chapter Three in *Feelings Buried Alive Never Die* . . . .

CHAPTER 2

How We "Mis-Place" Our Identity

Do not weep; do not wax indignant.
Understand.

—Spinoza

What is the basis of our inherent essence? Who are we at our core? Has something happened to our true identity? If so, where did it go? How did we lose touch with it? How can we get it back? Have you ever asked yourself these questions?

When we are born, we are *Love*. We arrive here as *pure, innocent, accepting, loving, forgiving* and as *teachable* as is possible. This is our *true*, inherent, *Divine* nature—our *core* identity. This is registered in the "memory of perfection" in our DNA. We are all beautiful children of God and we carry His characteristics within us.

As babies and young children we automatically exhibit this loving, accepting, and forgiving nature. We don't even have to try to be that way. We just are. Someone made the observation that if we would let our newborn children learn from other young children instead of adults, they would be much better off.

So what happens? How do we "mis-place" this inherent identity? How does it end up "missing"? Where does it go?

When we begin growing and attempting to navigate in this world, it becomes necessary for us to make decisions and choices. Just crawling around as babies we begin investigating our world at that level. Sometimes our investigation meets with Mom's approval, and sometimes it doesn't. If we are told "No, no," and our hands are swatted, we have a decision to make before we try the same thing again. Do we chance having our hands swatted or do we forget about investigating that same object and go for something else? With each choice we make we have an experience. No matter how seemingly insignificant, each experience makes an impression upon our young mind.

Very early in life we also observe what is happening around us. Our mind (the thinking and perceiving part of consciousness: intellect or intelligence, according to the dictionary) is forever attempting to make sense of any disorder or incongruent behavior we see, whether between older siblings or between the adults in our life.

There is an internal meter in each one of us that resonates positively or negatively with everything happening around us. Whatever the age, at some level we pick up whether a situation is good or not so good—we feel it. However, inasmuch as we have no mature reference point, untangling the inconsistencies and confusions of life and making sense of our surroundings can be extremely challenging for our tender mind. Nevertheless, unconsciously we still attempt understanding and interpreting our experiences and the circumstances that surround us.

Eventually, whether correct or incorrect, our own unique perception of each incident we encounter or observe evolves. Upon the establishment of a perception, the nature of the mind is to draw a conclusion for the purpose of navigating and surviving. The only problem is, although innocently formulated in our subconscious, the conclusions are often erroneous. But we don't know that. Nonetheless, our view of life and how to play the game of life is determined through the eyes of these perceptions. A perfect example is when a new baby is born into a family. Often the sibling just older than the baby feels replaced, rejected, or less loved than before. Or, they may feel they're not important or that they don't matter anymore.

Under extreme conditions, the conclusions formulated from our perceptions are more significantly impacted. In an abusive environment of any kind, the input into the formulation of these conclusions is predominantly negative and incongruent. Consequently, a disjointed or irrational view of life is created. As one of my clients, who has experienced the worst kind of abuse, describes it

> When a care giver gives wrong information to a child, the mind/body system automatically reacts to the misinformation as a trauma. The child doesn't arrive at conclusions, it is given conclusions. The information given doesn't match what the mind/body of the child would naturally rely on for survival—the child's innate instincts and formative learning experiences. They have been discounted and ridiculed. For example: A little girl is wearing wool pants, ironed on an asbestos ironing board which causes severe skin irritation that feels terrible. She squirms and complains. Her parents tell

her, It's all in your head. (You don't really feel what you feel!) This is "wrong" information.

Another example is when a parent says, "You kids drive me crazy." Then the child feels responsible for the parent's mental state and well-being. This is far too much responsibility to put on a young child. It distorts their sense of reality— their *true* sense of control. On the one hand they are told they don't know what they are talking about (the pants don't itch), while on the other hand they supposedly have all this power and control—enough to "drive their parents crazy." Having these inconsistencies thrown at them often enough creates major confusion in their minds. Consequently, they usually come to feel that they can't do anything right and/or that they are the cause of everything bad in the world. The child's perception of the degree of control they can exercise over their environment becomes more and more warped.

Parents who deny and distort a child's pain and reality in this way do it again and again. The trauma gets multiplied a hundred or a thousand times. The "wrong" information splits the child's connection with her own self—her own senses and intuition. This is deeply traumatic.

Who can the child now rely on? The adult caregiver who offers only pain? The adult who shames the child for feeling pain? Her traumatized, split self? When the child goes out into the world, he or she will only be able to do so with intense fear and shame. With no healthy self (feelings, sensations, natural instincts, and intuition) to guide him or her. He or she is familiar only with pain and shame and therefore finds or attracts only those who continue perpetuating this pain and shame.

This person will have very little free choice unless he or she becomes aware of how he or she has been limited by early experiences and eventually becomes healed.

When the above scenario is present, we decide very quickly that life is unsafe, unfair, and has no rhyme or reason. We are victims of those in charge of us and we feel powerless to satisfy them. Sometimes the abuse is purposeful, but often those responsible don't even realize they are being abusive. Their behavior is merely reactive, reflecting their own early conditioning. Nevertheless, in such circumstances just surviving each day without someone's wrath takes all the energy we have. As a result of the abuse, we are in a constant state of alertness in order to survive. Our bodies become machines, automatically reacting. Consequently, we don't experience life the way others do. Essentially, we have been forced to forfeit our agency, our will. The option for choices is completely closed off. Our conditioned reactions become firmly embedded in us and keep driving our behavior, even when the conditions may have changed. Often there are no resources left within us to learn anything different, because our *agency*—our ability to freely *choose*—is no longer intact.

Because the mind has to do something with the information it collects, our confusion or incorrect perceptions (from our feelings) and their subsequent conclusions (our thoughts, attitudes, and beliefs) run our life! If we have suffered abuse, the effect often takes the form of allowing someone else to run our life. As abused individuals, we often had strict obedience imposed upon us. Because we have not been free to think for ourselves, we sometimes become perfect candidates for joining any movement or cause that might come along. We may also be drawn to cults or leaders who seem to have all the answers. Our ability to sift true information from untrue information is greatly impaired.

But it is not only the abused who are susceptible to having others run their lives. If an individual has not been allowed to express what they feel or think, if their parents have not validated them in their feelings and intuition, and if strict obedience was demanded, this individual seldom has a sense of their *Self.* Consequently, they could be candidates for conditioning of the mind and emotions which can be accomplished by some religious or other organized groups. This conditioning can also be achieved by the media, certain entertainment, and some books. The conditioning can be so effective that often people have a difficult time thinking for themselves.

Regardless of previous circumstances, the psyche (the conscious and the unconscious together as a unit) continues to categorize and file all the information it gathers. Whenever our feelings are hurt or we are mistreated in any way, we know something is amiss. Due to our conditioned or still immature reference point, we seldom understand how to cope with that hurt or mistreatment. Consequently, it's impossible to resolve the hurt or be at peace with it in our feeling nature. So, without our consciously knowing it, somewhere inside of us that hurt is stored. It continually waits to be acknowledged and honored by being re-solved. This, coupled with the incongruent behavior we see in the adults around us, causes major confusion and inner conflict. Something inside is saying, "Wait a minute. This isn't what I learned and understood before I came here!" Nevertheless, we have to go on living.

Ranae Johnson, author and developer of *Rapid Eye Therapy,* explains it this way. Human instinct is to release emotions [feelings/thoughts] when they occur—like a baby screaming to be fed, or a child crying when it is hurt. However, spontaneous reactions to trauma are often invalidated or not tolerated by others, and eventually we ourselves disallow it. We don't want to be considered a cry baby, naughty, or whatever. By the time we reach adulthood, our conditioning has been to repress, store, trap, or deny our responses to negative experiences. These original emotional responses and any internal messages created at the time (Everyone is more important than I am) are still stored somewhere inside until we are able to identify, address, and release them in a meaningful way. This phenomenon is usually the root of much of the dis-ease in our bodies. And, I might add, it is the root of much of the emotional dysfunction in our lives as well.

Meanwhile, whatever our circumstances, the process of accumulating attitudes and beliefs based on our perceptions continues. While this is transpiring, our internal map for traveling our road of life is being established. Naturally, our journey is governed by this map; and we travel the road accordingly, gathering data from our experiences as we go. Our mind places this data in files (the brain) for future reference. For instance, if somewhere along our road an incident occurs that causes us to feel vulnerable and helpless, this data is filed. Each time our feeling nature senses the approach of a similar incident, it whips back to the file with corresponding data and instantly decides how to deal with it. An immediate natural response is to defend or protect the *Self*. Consequently, a defense mechanism is automatically put in place.

One such mechanism is the construction of a psychological wall. Each time our feelings overwhelm us or hurt so much that we don't even care to feel anymore, a block is added to the wall and the wall becomes taller and wider. Eventually our feelings turn off. The wall is stopping the flow of energy necessary to keep us balanced and moving forward. It contributes to an eventual breakdown of our physical, emotional, or spiritual health. Major dysfunction can be the result.

Another factor worth considering in this equation is that we inherit unresolved feelings, attitudes, and beliefs our ancestors have unknowingly shared with us through their/our DNA. These energies also have a definite impact on us in the overall picture. As a result, we may not be dealing with just our own "stuff" as we are striving to heal. (Thank you Mom, Dad, Grandma, Grandpa, Great-Grandma, and Great-Grandpa! You are helping me discover who I am.)

The perfect blueprint in our DNA is composed of light—Divine light—which is a powerful frequency. Since feelings also possess a frequency, every time we experience a negative feeling (or frequency) it acts like a short in our electrical system. The light becomes dimmer. Bit by bit these negative feelings obscure or even turn off our light, thereby diminishing and diluting the *Love* that we are. We may not be aware that this is happening. We may not even realize that we have a Divine nature or that we *are* Love. Nonetheless, one step at a time our Divine nature is replaced by what eventually becomes a counterfeit nature. And while our core identity is being eroded, confusion and inner conflict build inside us. Could this have anything to do with the lack of inner peace in our society?

Our natural, unconscious drive is to re-turn to and re-claim the beautiful, inherent Divine qualities that we carry within ourselves. Yes . . . they are still in the memory of perfection of our DNA. Unbeknown to us, these qualities have been obscured by inharmonious feelings and thoughts, or someone's erroneous use of will throughout our life. Subconsciously, our major objective is to re-call and re-connect with our basic glorious qualities—the ones we brought with us when we were born.

Even though we can accomplish this re-connection at any segment of our life's journey, our choices determine when this takes place. If our wisdom allows us to see the picture before the twilight years of our life, we don't have to be old before accomplishing our re-union. The road continues on and on, even after we re-connect with the Truth of our Be-ing.

In the Bible (King James version), we are told in Matthew 18:3-4, ". . . Verily I say unto you, Except ye be converted, and become as little children, ye shall not enter into the kingdom of heaven. Whosoever therefore shall humble himself as this little child, the same is greatest in the kingdom of heaven." And in Mark 10:15 it says, "Verily I say unto you, Whosoever shall not receive the kingdom of God as a little child, he shall not enter therein." How can we be like a little child if we aren't one? Could it be as simple as re-turning to the Love that we are? But how do we do that?

CHAPTER 3

Come With Me On a Journey

The longest journey is the journey inwards...
—Dag Hammarskjold

In August of 1991, *Feelings Buried Alive Never Die . . .* was published. Shortly thereafter I started receiving requests to do seminars and workshops, with the book as the focus. I had anticipated the possibility of this happening and had some idea of what it would entail. For several years prior to this I had conducted various kinds of seminars and workshops, primarily having to do with self-improvement. I truly enjoy both teaching and assisting people in seeing the beauty of their soul. So when the occasion presented itself to create a workshop with the book as the subject matter, I was eager to respond. I felt there was a lot that could be done in this setting which would give people an opportunity to better connect with their feelings, thereby enhancing what they learned from the book.

I am the type of person who sincerely desires being the instrument God would have me be; I sought direction from

Him as to how to structure this workshop. When the direction came it was in the form of an illustration, complete with the main dialogue.

I was shown that each of us had a very straight road extending in front of us as we entered this earthly sphere. We each, one at a time, stood at the beginning of this road—our road of life—and questions were asked: Did you come with a road map for your journey through life? Did a book of instructions or directions come with you as you arrived—one that you had in your hands and could read for yourself?" Of course the answers were, No."

Without knowing it, our biggest challenge while traveling our individual road is to keep from taking a detour, which is what happened to me the moment I was born! No one was there to welcome me to earth. This told me I'm not important, and it was internalized as true. At that point, "I'm not important" became the main detour upon which I traveled for the next 48 years. (Covered in more detail on page 101 of *Feelings Buried Alive Never Die . . .*)

You may already realize you have been on a detour, or are still on one. Understand that a detour was taken the moment an untruth about your *Self* was perceived and believed, or the moment you experienced negative feelings or negative thoughts toward someone else. Why did this put you on a detour? Because it took you from the Love that you are—the straight road in front of you. The instant negativity takes you out of harmony with God's laws, i.e. "Love thy neighbor as thyself," or "Do unto others as you would have them do unto you," you are off on another road.

Without our realizing it, when incorrect perceptions,

misguided feelings, thoughts, attitudes and beliefs occur, we have taken a definite detour from our designated road of Love. Could it be that many of us are out there traveling around on detours, trying to figure out how the heck to get back to our main road?

Unfortunately (or so it seems), while on this detour we encounter bumps and boulders which cause us to stumble and sometimes fall. When we tire of going around these obstructions and the inconvenience they cause, we may become aware that the obstructions are there for a reason. Could they be indicating something to us? Perhaps their existence is to get our attention—to help us "wake up" from our slumber. They may be a warning to assist us in seeing that our perceptions, feelings, thoughts, and attitudes need re-directing or re-shaping. As we become aware of the true significance of our challenges, we can allow the bumps and boulders to assist us in re-turning to our designated road.

While striving to understand why undesirable circum-stances are presented to us, if we look within (introspect) and observe our own mental processes, it is possible—with some effort—to improve our state of affairs. By introspect-ing we may discover if we have been conditioned or have innocently allowed our *Self* to experience undesirable results in our life. It's only by looking inside our *Self* that we gain insight into the causes of these unfavorable effects.

By being open to learning what makes us tick, we dis-cover more and more about our *Self* and eventually find the answers we are seeking. For instance: We may desire finan-cial abundance, and work and work to make it happen, but we just seem to be spinning our wheels. This could go on for years. With introspection we may come to realize that we know too many people who are financially well-to-do, but are very dishonest. For some reason this could indicate to us, on a subconscious level, that we have to be dishonest in order to experience abundance. If our nature is to be honest and uncompromising in our values, subconsciously we may feel we don't want to take the risk of being that kind of person. We would rather not have abundance than compromise our values. This constitutes a belief which we unknowingly established from our perceptions. It is there before we can do anything about it, and it creates a block to our experiencing abundance. We could compare it to crazy wiring in a house, where the light switches don't turn on the right lights. We may *think* we desire abundance, but we don't *feel* it; consequently, we are being double-minded. And our feelings always win.

Here is a side note that you might find interesting. In 1998 I attended a three-week retreat in Vancouver, B.C., Canada, the name of which was *Seeing Without Glasses*, directed by Dr. Robert-Michael Kaplan. The retreat was for the purpose of learning about the physical, nutritional, and emotional aspects of the eyes.

This particular science has always interested me and I felt a strong desire to absorb all I could. I took the opportunity offered at the retreat, not only to learn but to enjoy the beautiful setting of the Sunshine Coast. The retreat consisted of nearly 70 hours of class and study time each week, which was not only intense but also extremely stimulating and nourishing in many ways. We were taught about all the intricacies of the eyes and their functions. Naturally I was greatly interested in the emotional indicators and how they are represented in the eyes.

Dr. Kaplan taught us about the *fovea* and the *retina* of the eye and how closely related they are—the fovea layering right behind the retina when in its perfect state, the two working in tandem. His concern was that more and more people are experiencing a separation between the retina and the fovea of their eyes, which causes a definite and specific need for glasses and sometimes creates other serious problems, as well.

The significance of this phenomenon is that the *retina* represents our *feelings* and the *fovea* represents our *thinking*. Those of you who have read *Feelings Buried Alive Never Die* . . . will remember that when our thinking and feeling are not in "sync," we are double-minded; and the feelings (registered in the subconscious) always override the thinking. (We may *think* we would like prosperity or friends, but if we don't *feel* worthy or acceptable, our *feelings* dictate the outcome.) In other words, according to Dr. Kaplan's findings, the double-mindedness in the world today is being created because our feelings and thoughts are becoming more divergent, incongruent, and farther apart. His concern is the same as mine—that we begin understanding the importance of Be-ing congruent in everything we feel and think, and then, in everything we say and do. In other words, we cannot feel one thing, think another, then say and do yet another.

It is by having our feelings in alignment with our thoughts that we create the reality we desire so that life subsequently works for us. And, who knows, our eyes may get better too. (See Chapter 5 in *Feelings Buried Alive Never Die* . . . for further understanding of this principle.)

*The reference point from which I view the world
determines how things present themselves to me.*

Back to our road. By becoming more aware during our
life's journey, we eventually realize that our experiences
are for the purpose of teaching us about our *Self.* We learn
the lessons we came here to learn through our challenges in
these major areas: our relationships, our health, our children,
our finances. Someone once asked me, "How about all of the
above?" Sometimes it is all of the above, but most often we
find that one or two of these areas are our greatest tutor(s).
Our experiences in all of these areas serve as mirrors, reflecting back to us the issues we need to re-solve in order to more
fully understand and know our True Self.

When you begin recognizing the feelings, thoughts,
attitudes, and behavior that complicated your life, you
begin bringing your *Self* back to your main road. By focusing your awareness—accepting responsibility and accountability—you can continue your journey on this healing road.
As you travel, sooner or later you may come to a door. This
is a very significant door, as it allows you entrance to the
Truth of your Be-ing. When you reach this door you have
the opportunity of entering it and re-uniting with your
True Self—the one you forgot when you came to this
sphere. However, the only way to access this door is by
opening it from the inside—*from inside your Self.* And *you*
must be the one to do it; no one else can do it for you.

Each of us has an inborn, unconscious drive to re-
connect with our Divine energy—our accepting, forgiving,
genuinely sacred and loving heart—our True Self.

Somewhere along the course of our journey, we *can* re-discover who we really are.

If we are interested in re-uniting with the Love that we are, a clean-up campaign may be in order. This is called cleansing the inner vessel. What is meant by "cleansing the inner vessel"? It means achieving a change of mind—a change of *heart*. We cleanse (adjust, alter, or bring into alignment) our inner vessel by healing negative feelings, thoughts, and attitudes; by re-moving the obstacles that originated from our innocent, inaccurate perceptions, mis-guided conclusions, and early conditioning. We cleanse our inner vessel by establishing a fresh view about ourselves, God, life, the world, and others. And no matter how we've been "wired up" inside our *Self*, it's okay. Whatever we've done, it's okay. It just "is." If we don't like how it is, with some effort we can change it.

Recognizing, identifying, and re-solving that which has been repressed is necessary in cleansing the inner vessel. This is only accomplished, however, through conscious effort (which eventually becomes "effortless" effort). *Awareness* is the key. By beginning from the inside—from our *feelings*, from our *heart*—and then working outward, this cleansing can take place.

As we cleanse the inner vessel by removing what has been covering our Inner Light, we are preparing for the re-establishment of the beautiful qualities deep inside us. We are preparing to find that part of our *Self* which we have forgotten—our True Self, our Divine Self. Many of these qualities have been suppressed throughout our life due to our conditioned need to make everyone happy, to keep peace at all costs, to be accepted and, above all, to conform.

Heaven forbid that we should be unique or different!

I found a story recently on the internet that beautifully illustrates what unknowingly happens to us on our journey.

In that place between wakefulness and dreams, I found myself in a room. There were no distinguishing features in this room save the one wall covered with small index card files. They were like the ones in libraries that list titles by author or subject in alphabetical order. But these files, which stretched from floor to ceiling and were seemingly endless in either direction, had very different headings. As I drew near the wall of files, the first to catch my attention was the one that read "Girls I Have Liked." I opened it and began flipping through the cards. I quickly shut it, shocked to realize that I recognized the names written on each one.

And then without being told, I knew exactly where I was. This lifeless form with its small files was a crude catalog system for my life. Here were written the actions of every moment, big and small, in a detail my memory couldn't match.

A sense of wonder and curiosity, coupled with humor, stirred within me as I began randomly opening files and exploring their content. Some brought joy and sweet memories, others a sense of shame and a shudder to see if anyone was watching.

A file named "Friends" was next to one marked "Friends I Have Betrayed!"

The titles ranged from the mundane to the outright weird. "Books I Have Read." "Lies I Have Told." "Comfort I Have Given." "Jokes I Have Laughed At." Some were almost hilarious in their exactness. "Things I've Yelled at My Brothers." Others I couldn't laugh at: "Things I Have Done in My Anger." "Things I Have Muttered Under My Breath to

My Parents." I never ceased to be surprised by the contents. Often there were many more cards than I expected. Sometimes fewer than I had hoped.

I was overwhelmed by the sheer volume of the life I had lived. Could it be possible that I had the time in my 40 years to write this truth? Each was written in my own handwriting. Each signed with my own signature.

When I pulled out the file marked "Songs I Have Listened To," I realized the file grew to contain its contents. The cards were packed tightly, and yet after two or three years, I hadn't found the end of the file. I shut it, shamed, not so much by the quality of the music, but more by the vast amount of time I knew that file represented.

When I came to a file marked "Lustful Thoughts," I felt a chill run through my body. I pulled the card file out only an inch, not willing to test its size, and drew out a card. I shuddered at its detailed content. I felt sick to think that such a moment had been recorded.

An almost animal rage broke on me. One thought dominated my mind: "No one must ever see these cards! No one must ever see this room! I have to destroy them!" In an insane frenzy I yanked the file out. Its size didn't matter now. I had to empty it and burn the cards. But as I took it at one end and began pounding it on the floor, I could not dislodge a single card. I became desperate and pulled out a card, only to find it as strong as steel when I tried to tear it.

Defeated and utterly helpless, I returned the file to its slot. Leaning my forehead against the wall, I let out a long, self-pitying sigh. And then I saw it. The title—"People I Have Shared [Jesus' Teachings] With." The handle was brighter than those around it, newer, only inches long; it fell into my hands. I could count the cards it contained on one hand.

And then the tears came. I began to weep. Sobs so deep that the hurt started in my stomach and shot through me. I fell on my knees and cried. I cried from the overwhelming shame of it all. The rows of file shelves swirled in my tear-filled eyes. No one must ever, ever know of this room. I must lock it up and hide the key.

But then, as I pushed away the tears, I saw Him. No, please not Him. Not here. Oh, anyone but Jesus. I watched helplessly as he began to open the files and read the cards. I couldn't bear to watch the look on His face. I saw a sorrow deeper than my own. He seemed to intuitively go to the worst boxes. Why did He have to read every one?

Finally He turned and looked at me from across the room. He looked at me with pity in His eyes. But this was a pity that didn't anger me. I dropped my head, covered my face and began to cry again. He walked over and put His arm around me. He could have said so many things. But He didn't say a word. He just cried with me.

Then He got up and walked back to the wall of files. Starting at one end of the room He took out a file and one by one, began to sign His name over mine on each card.

"No!" I shouted, rushing at Him. All I could find to say was, "No, no" as I pulled a card from Him. His name shouldn't be on these cards. But there it was, written in red so rich, so dark, so alive. The name of Jesus covered mine.

It was written with His blood.

He gently took the card back. He smiled a sad smile and began to sign the cards. I don't think I'll ever understand how He did it so quickly, but the next instant it seemed I heard Him close the last file and said, "It is finished."

I stood up, and He let me out of the room. There was no lock on its door. There were still cards to be written.

—Unknown

Before I read the above, I had personal experiences with two people who had something similar happen to them: their feelings and thoughts were represented as cards in a stack, but for them, as they became accountable for their inharmonious feelings and Scripted to change them, those cards took wing and immediately disappeared from the stacks.

Just how important is it for our well-being to absolve ourselves of these old cards? Evidently a great deal of importance is placed upon it, as there are many references to our heart (where our feelings reside), our thoughts, and our words in the Bible. Also, a friend recently referred me to the *Gospel of Thomas* (from the ancient Nag Hammadi texts), where Christ says it perfectly: "If you bring forth what is within you, what you bring forth will save you. If you do not bring forth what is within you, what you do not bring forth will destroy you."

The purpose of conducting my original "Feelings Journey Workshops" was to assist people in understanding how they could begin to rid themselves of their cards—how they could bring forth what was within them, and set in motion the dismantling of their wall. When a person accepts responsibility for their feelings and thoughts, they usually desire doing whatever is necessary to align themselves with truth—the *truth about themselves*—because anytime we know the truth, it sets us free! Although it might be uncomfortable, most of us have been through worse, and the discomfort is only temporary. The clarity and understanding that follow are worth it all.

After choosing accountability for what they felt and thought, many workshop attendees utilized the Script for getting themselves off their detour and back to their main road. At the same time, they were also eliminating their cards, as well as chipping away at the blocks in the wall that represented their inharmonious feelings and thoughts. They were re-establishing harmony with God's laws—His laws of love, forgiveness, and restitution (the act of recovering a former state or posture).

With commitment and perseverance the inner vessel can be cleansed, the cards can be eliminated, the blocks removed from the wall. With the wall gone, the door is in front of you. All you have to do is take the necessary steps to open it so you can walk through and re-connect with the Love that you are.

Simultaneously, if we choose, we can support our inner cleansing by using the natural modalities God has placed here that help us in our healing and in changing from the outside in. Yes, these modalities have the ability to soothe, realign, and balance us. Some of them have the ability to alter our inner energies. However, it will still be necessary for you to deal with any resolution of feelings as well. That, as I mentioned, requires awareness and focused effort.

If you are interested in exploring the modalities I am referring to, they include aroma therapy (100% pure thera-peutic grade essential oils), art therapy, color therapy, energy therapy, flower remedies, gemstones, herbal therapy, mas-sage therapy, music therapy, sound/tone therapy, zone ther-apy, and other therapies you may have discovered for your-self that also aid in this cleansing.

If you have taken a detour from your unique road, applying the information contained in this book may assist you while you are:

1. Re-turning to your road,
2. Cleansing the inner vessel,
3. Eliminating your card files,
4. Dismantling the blocks of your wall,
5. Learning to *see* as you are *looking* for your True Self,
6. Healing Feelings . . . From Your Heart, and
7. Discovering your *Divine Self*—the Love that you are.

CHAPTER 4

Which One Needs Healing?

We are entering the dimension where we have control—
the inside.

—Byron Katie

The degree of success we experience when cleansing the inner vessel and re-connecting with our True Self is often commensurate with the amount of healing our Inner Child has experienced. When the major part of our hurt or pain is "stuck" in the *Child aspect* of us (and we rarely have a conscious understanding of where we are stuck), it can be challenging for us to forgive. This is because the Child is still reeling from the unresolved emotional pain experienced during childhood.

An individual may also be stuck in another aspect of their Be-ing, for along with the Child aspect we also have the aspects of our *Will, Self, Female, Male, Parent,* and *Adult*. Sometimes it is necessary to address the *Baby* or even the *Fetal* aspect of a person. In addition to the aspects, there are the *Physical, Mental, Emotional,* and *Spiritual areas* of the individual to consider.

As we know, each human being comes with their own unique personality, which is usually evident within days of their birth. As we also know, the development of each personality is decidedly affected by outside stimuli from a very early period of fetal development. Since each individual is unique in every way, several personalities (people) exposed to the same exact stimuli would be affected differently. In other words, what would bother one personality may not even make a ripple in another. It's just the way we are.

Currently I am working with Terah, a talented and brilliant ten-year-old girl whose parents have been at their wits end due to her seeming lack of common sense. She has a difficult time being responsible for anything—getting herself ready for school, bringing her assignments home, taking her puppy outside to relieve itself, giving her parents phone messages, remembering where she puts things, and so on. At present, Terah's seven-year-old sister is much more responsible than she. It is difficult for the parents to watch what Terah is going through at school, as well as at home. No one understands her or what makes her tick. She is unsure of herself and doesn't have many friends; connecting with another person is essentially impossible for her. Terah escapes reality by sitting for long periods in front of the television. Even though she is musically inclined (playing the violin and piano), practicing takes much more effort than she cares to put forth. Basically, it seems there is little joy in anything for Terah.

One day in talking with Marilyn, a colleague and friend, I mentioned the challenges Terah is facing. I shared with her some of the frustrating scenarios Terah's parents had recounted to me. Upon hearing these accounts

Marilyn suggested that Terah may be "stuck" in her Baby aspect, and that she needed to be nurtured, cuddled, and cared for as if she were a baby, with no expectations or pressures put upon her. When Marilyn offered this as a possibility, I knew it was true.

Marilyn then told me about an eight-year-old Native American girl she and her husband had adopted many years ago. During early childhood this girl had been left alone daily for hours at a time with her little brother. Consequently, the girl's development was dwarfed, due to the lack of nurturing, bonding, and love. As Marilyn prayed to know what to do and how to help this unfortunate child, it was conveyed to her that the adopted girl was stuck in her Baby aspect. Marilyn had received the guidance she suggested for Terah, to help the Native American girl "mature up" to her current age. Marilyn's husband and children worked as a team in helping this young girl move beyond her *Baby aspect*. After about two months of dedicated effort from the family, the girl outgrew her need to be nurtured and cuddled. She evolved into a normal member of Marilyn's family as the under-developed Baby aspect was finally contented and made whole from the loving therapy she received.

Upon hearing about Marilyn's experience, I was reminded of what had taken place when Terah was six weeks old. Her mother returned to teaching school because her father was finishing his education. Terah was taken to a baby sitter every morning. She would start crying the minute she was handed to the baby sitter and would cry practically all day. They went through five baby sitters in two months because no one could handle Terah's marathon crying. (And there's no telling what happened with the baby sitters.) Leaving her in someone else's care was extremely difficult for Terah's parents, but there were no other options if her father was to finish college.

Evidently being left with baby sitters was so emotionally traumatic for Terah that that part of her—that *aspect*—had never healed. Because of her experiences she is still stuck in the first few months of her life. Even now, when a situation presents itself that Terah has a difficult time handling, she takes a hike, so to speak. She checks out because it's too painful to stay in the present situation. She reverts to the only way she has known for dealing with a challenge—essentially the same way she dealt with being left by her mom and dad. Checking out was her mechanism for survival as a baby and continues to be as a ten-year-old. At present she is being nurtured, cuddled, and having the Baby aspect of her needs filled at home.

Another technique Terah's mother is using involves sitting face to face with her, silently and lovingly holding her hands. They look into each other's eyes, keeping continuous, unbroken contact without distractions. They will do this 15 minutes each day for at least six consecutive days. Terah will then repeat the process with her dad. If the parents can send forth, from their hearts, loving messages to Terah while in this process, the therapy will be even more effective. This exercise will help create the bonding between Terah and her parents that didn't occur during birth, due to complications, and which were later compounded by mom having to leave daily.

Terah is also using the Script with me to process the feelings she has never been able to verbalize. These include feeling abandoned, rejected, angry, betrayed, alone, hopeless, helpless, mom wasn't there for me, and no one cares.

Another aspect of Terah that has been affected by this very early trauma in her life is her Will, which was clearly but unavoidably taken from her. Although she had no say in the situation, she certainly didn't want her mom and dad to leave her every day. Unfortunately, these things happen daily, everywhere, without mal-intent. Often they cannot be avoided. However, now that we better understand how a child can be affected at such an early age, perhaps we as parents can be more sensitive to what our children may have lacked or missed during their early years. Now we can strive to remedy and heal it.

Children reach out for healing in the most interesting ways. Most of the time they reach out by their behavior. If there seems to be something "wrong" with a child, there is usually an underlying reason for the behavior. The reason needs to be discovered and addressed in a loving manner. The greatest crime of all (short of murder) is to turn the mind of a child against him or herself. Blaming or shaming a child out of their behavior only leaves gaping wounds that will eventually need to be healed, and perhaps even require therapy.

If a parent has no idea of what to look for or how to remedy a child's behavior, patience and prayer is a good place to start. We don't have to be all alone in deciding on a course of action. There is always help close at hand. When God knows that we are sincerely seeking answers, He will respond. It might not be immediately, but if we ask long enough—not just with our lips, but sincerely and from our heart—we *will* receive the answers. In the meantime, consistently applying some of these suggested processes or techniques may be appropriate and helpful.

Sometimes a challenge can go even deeper than the Baby aspect. The Fetal aspect of a person may need to be addressed. This can be a very interesting aspect as there are people who have had significant intrauterine trauma. Many stories can be told of what happens in a small percentage of pregnancies—of the "missing twin"—with the multiple fetuses that never fully developed. Imprinted in the DNA memory of the surviving child is the knowledge of a missing brother or sister. There is an earthly feeling of loss, grief, or dis-connectedness that may be difficult to overcome.

I have worked with several people who brought unfinished business with them from their fetal journey as a result of the missing twin. Some of them had serious traumatic feelings to resolve. Their experiences were very powerful and profound, but that's an entirely different book.

In the work I do, experience has shown that often a person holds or harbors their unresolved feelings in two or three of the areas or aspects of themselves at the same time. (I call these feelings, *voices.*) So a person can simultaneously be stuck in their Child, Female, and Will (or in other aspects), as well as in the Emotional and/or Mental or Spiritual areas of their Be-ing. If a person isn't aware of the voices that represent their feelings in these areas and aspects, the voices can't be addressed. These voices may eventually show up in the *Physical* area, manifesting themselves as gall stones, cancer, liver, kidney, or heart problems, or other "dis-eases" and conditions.

These hurting voices, however, desire to be acknowledged and dealt with so that effective healing can occur. And the areas and aspects of our True Self desire to be discovered by one another so they can re-solve old pain; so they can once again come together as a whole and re-connect with the Truth of our Be-ing. Some of these voices have been waiting a long time for recognition and rescue, for being liberated from their prison.

How do these voices come to reside in the different areas and aspects of a person?

As children, regardless of age, each time our *Will* is broken or dishonored—each time we are distraught or unjustly disciplined, humiliated or hurt (no matter the severity of the hurt)—if we have no recourse nor the the ability to resolve the incident, the area and aspect being affected literally freezes in time, as with Terah. Yes, the unresolved feelings from traumatic incidents freeze somewhere in our Be-ing, affecting not only our emotional health, but eventually our physical as well (perhaps our liver stomach, throat, or spleen). As a result, areas and aspects of us have been waiting, perhaps years, for the opportunity to heal the emotional and physical pain of these stored or buried unresolved feelings.

When the hurting voices are not recognized, the negative energy of the feelings they represent compounds, and continues compounding until it can no longer be contained in our "inner chambers." If this negative energy is not resolved, it eventually works its way into the physical body—chemistry, tissue, blood, and muscles—in order to finally get our attention. If we go too long without a resolution, our mental state is also affected.

Throughout our life, events occur that throw us back into or trigger some of those same old unresolved feelings, at which point we become the three-year-old again, or the eight-year-old, or the twelve-year-old—whatever age we were when that feeling froze in time. Perhaps it was the two-year-old who had his Will taken from him, or the eight-year-old who had her intent questioned, or the ten-year-old who had his intelligence or reasoning criticized or ridiculed.

Situations may occur over and over throughout our life which resonate or reconnect us with one of our old frozen feelings. Who knows how many of them we have. No matter what our age when one of these old feelings is triggered by someone or something, we automatically and instantly revert to the age or the time when the feeling was established. When this happens we literally take on the emotional demeanor of the age at which the feelings froze. Stated another way, the sub-conscious mind re-acts at the age the feeling was stored. Have you ever reacted strongly to someone or something and wondered where in the world that reaction came from?

How do we know which "voices" need healing?

Each uncomfortable feeling, each conflicting feeling, each less than glorious feeling, each feeling that takes you out of peace is a voice in your emotional nature. When I say voice, I am referring to an unpleasant feeling that keeps re-occurring. This voice is crying out to be heard so that it can be acknowledged, achieve resolution, and be healed.

Our everyday feelings and any negative behavior they give rise to are the most glaring indicators of being stuck in a frozen state, stuck in our ability to progress! This is why becoming consciously aware of what we feel inside is so immeasurably important to cultivate on a daily basis. Becoming acutely aware of our feelings is also paramount if we expect to make effective changes for moving out of our old behavior patterns.

How, then, do we know what we are feeling?

The answer is simple. Inasmuch as most of us have not been taught to pay attention to what we say, we are rather mindless and unconscious of the *words* we use. Seldom do we *consciously* hear what our lips are *speaking*. However sad, but true, the majority of us have not been encouraged during childhood to recognize or identify the feelings that dwell inside us. So the *first* indicator, and best place for starting our quest in recognizing these feelings, is with our words. We begin by listening to our words, and then move inward.

How many of us weigh our words before we say them? How often do we really listen to what we actually say? Most of the time we just say the first thing that pops into our mind. Realize, however, that what we speak is the most obvious and audible indicator of what we are feeling. So this is the best place for beginning our journey inward—by listening to the words that come out of our mouth. When listening to what we say, we hear some of the strongest clues to what we are truly feeling, particularly if we tend to be verbose. Therefore, if we are having a difficult time tuning in to our feelings, by listening to the words we speak, we hear the first indicators of our feelings.

Keep in mind that every word we speak is a message or command to the universe. And what we say with feeling and with repetition we do create—desirable or undesirable. So, by diligently listening to our own words, this new awareness, and the attention we are finally giving our words, allows them to be at our conscious command.

We can be the master of our words, rather than remaining their unconscious slave. When we are the master, our words can be the greatest ally we may ever discover.

By recognizing our outer-talk and its link to our feelings (observing how it impacts our daily life) we are prepared for pinpointing what goes on inside our head. Hence, by listening to our words—our outer-talk—we are training ourselves to take the next step in discovering our feelings.

The *second* indicator of what we truly feel inside is our inner-talk; or, as it is generally called, our self-talk—that dialogue constantly going on inside our head of which we are usually unaware. Many of us are afraid to speak out loud what we would like to say. Therefore, the conversations stay inside our head. The major problem is that these conversations are rather one-sided. Unless we pay close attention to what we are saying, our imagination can run away with us and eventually create mountains out of mole hills.

These conversations that we carry on within our *Self* can either bring us down or pull us up. We *do* have a choice in the matter. Before we can do anything about it we must discover what we are saying inside our head.

Thus far, most of us probably haven't paid much attention to these inside discussions—to our self-talk. Developing the ability to *listen* to and *hear* these conversations is deeply revealing and a vital step in moving for-

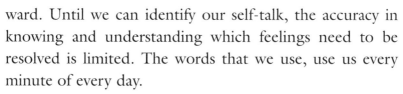

ward. Until we can identify our self-talk, the accuracy in knowing and understanding which feelings need to be resolved is limited. The words that we use, use us every minute of every day.

Listen and hear how you really see your *Self* and life around you. Inasmuch as you are continually gathering information on what makes you tick and constantly discovering what you feel when you listen, your self-talk is one of your best guides for becoming better acquainted with you.

By actively paying attention to your outer-talk and your self-talk, you become equipped for discovering the *third* indicator of your feelings—your *thoughts*. After acquiring the skill of listening and identifying your self-talk, tuning in to what you are thinking is simple—but extremely necessary. Nevertheless, there is a fine line between *thoughts* and *self-talk*. For the purposes of this book, *thought* is used as defined in *Noah Webster's 1828 American Dictionary of the English Language*. It means "inward reasoning; the working of conscience." (I use this vintage dictionary as I feel it provides the more accurate and original meaning of words).

Thoughts are more subtle and require constant vigilance if one is to remain aware of them. Thoughts reveal our feelings; they are also very useful in letting us know what needs changing or healing. *Be aware that feelings are usually expressed through our thoughts before we ever speak.* Connecting with our thoughts first, however, is sometimes a challenge—especially if we don't talk much.

Thoughts, being more subtle than expressed words, are sometimes more difficult to *hear*—or tune in to.

Taking it a step at a time: if we are not aware of what is taking place inwardly with our feelings, by the time our thoughts indicate what we are feeling, our feelings and thoughts have combined together and become *e-motion* (energy in motion) and are manifested in our re-actions. Feeling+thought=e-motion, energy-in-motion. Subsequently, in the natural course of events, our emotion further expresses itself through our *attitudes* and *beliefs*, which are then externalized and manifested through our *actions* and *behavior.* This all happens in less than a split second.

Therefore, it is useful to direct your consciousness to your thought processes as much as possible. Be observant and mindful of the thoughts that pop into your mind in connection with your feeling nature. Each time you are surprised by your thoughts toward someone or something, ask yourself, Where did that come from? Trace the thought back to where it seemed to be triggered. What did someone say or do to cause the thought? By developing an aptitude in training your thoughts you enhance your ability to look within, thereby gaining a deeper understanding of your *Self.*

Keep in mind that thoughts will also "come into your mind" in the form of ideas or impressions, perhaps directing you in your work or day-to-day activities. By being aware of these thoughts, as well as the thoughts relating to your emotional nature, you can become truly adept at recognizing a unique part of your human nature. It's like getting to know a whole new person.

When you are in tune with your words, your self-talk, and your thoughts, you ultimately become skillful in making that most elusive of connections—the connection with your *feelings*. Besides your feelings manifesting in your words, self-talk, and thoughts, your body will give you clues as well. Be aware of any inward change of body comfort (jaw tightening, blood pressure rising, body heat, face flushing, etc.) while conversing with someone or participating in activities with people. Pay attention to your body movements and your body language. Something as simple as not being able to look a person in the eye while you're talking to them tells you something.

Feelings can be very challenging to identify and perhaps the most difficult part of this whole equation to uncover. Because our feelings reside so deeply inside us and we haven't been tutored in recognizing or appropriately expressing them, un-covering these feelings may be a whole new experience for some. Be assured, though, that it can be done.

Keep in mind the useful indicators, heretofore mentioned, that greatly benefit you while un-covering your feelings. In fact, mindfulness is the key. Be-ing consciously aware of the indicators of your feelings is what it's all about. So be willing to spend the necessary time required for attaining this awareness. Be eager to spend silent time—going within—listening to your *Self*.

Bridging the gap from your *unknown* feelings to your *known* feelings can be exciting! It only requires spending time to cultivate your ability to recognize the indicators of your words, self-talk, thoughts, and feelings—doing it one step at a time. Eventually you will become very proficient at identifying all your feelings.

To recap, as you master

1) *Listening* to your words—to your outer talk—you are training your *Self* for taking the next step, which is;
2) *Listening* to and *hearing* what you are saying to your *Self*—your self-talk. You then discover the passageway to your
3) *Thoughts.* By recognizing your thoughts you can begin tracing them back to
4) *Feelings,* which initially triggered the thoughts in the first place.

Even though we seem to think our thoughts before we feel our feelings, feelings are what originally caused the establishment of our thoughts, and eventually the two can work in tandem. It might sound complicated, but it really isn't. If you need further clarification or understanding, reviewing pages 7-8 and Chapter Six in *Feelings Buried Alive Never Die . . .* may be helpful.

Becoming skillful at listening to your outer and your inner-talk is the main point to remember. Eventually you will recognize your thoughts *before* they are born as words. Upon doing this you become friends with the feelings indicators. You can then zero in on negative feelings and nip them in the bud—before they are manifest as thoughts or words.

Following is an exercise that can sharpen your ability to be more objective with your inner world. During your daily activities, see your *Self* sitting in an auditorium as part of an audience watching your *Self* in a play—noticing everything you are saying and doing. Then observe your reactions and your feelings while doing this. By observing from the unique vantage point of the audience, you are decidedly more objective, for subconsciously you are not as emotionally involved. You are learning much more about your *Self* by Be-ing the spectator rather than the participant; by Be-ing the author rather than the actor. From this vantage point you can write your own lines and specify what takes place. You don't have to re-act. All you simply do is shift your *view* point.

You've heard it said that if you can change your thoughts, you can change your *Self*. As you now understand, it goes much deeper than that. When you go to the core and change what you feel (because your feelings are the heart and core of your emotions, thoughts, self-talk, and words), your thoughts automatically change—as does your self-talk.

Inasmuch as your feelings are the gateway to your spiritual self—your True Self—somewhere, sometime, sooner or later, changing your negative feelings will be a very high priority in your life. As you embrace truth with the desire of observing correct principles ("Love thy neighbor as thyself," and "Do unto others as you would have them do unto you"), you will understand how absolutely essential it is for you to Be aware of what you feel inside in order to remove your *Self* from your rut. Instead of fighting change or denying ownership of what you feel, identify and allow the feeling without being fearful. By doing this you take a quantum leap forward. Whereas, when you fear the feeling, you allow it to own and dominate you.

With understanding and the tools for discovering and healing each un-resolved feeling, you can take care of unfinished business, thereby moving forward on your journey to emotional wholeness. It is not necessary to be consciously aware of the areas or aspects undesirable feelings come from. The important thing is to change these feelings so their energy constrictions can be removed. This is the way healing—physically, mentally, emotionally *and* spiritually—takes place.

One of the most effective ways to resolve undesirable feelings and bring about desired changes is by addressing your feelings with the Script. Why? The Script addresses each and every level (your pre-earth experiences), each and every layer (all the layers of negative feelings accumulated in your DNA throughout your life), and each and every area (the physical, mental, emotional and spiritual) and aspect (the Child, Will, Self, Female, Male, Parent and Adult) of your Be-ing. Scripting does this without the necessity of you knowing *where* the feelings originated.

An important fundamental principle to keep in mind is that the longer you live and the older you become without the resolution of your emotional pain, the more pronounced the energy constrictions become. (See Chapter 13 in *Feelings Buried Alive Never Die* . . .)

Now you can better understand the importance of uncovering and re-solving your discordant feelings and thoughts. They do not belong to the Truth of your Be-ing. When these feelings and thoughts were created they had to go somewhere, so little by little they displaced your original positive feelings. Consequently, inner conflicts were created, the negative feelings being at odds with the positive feelings. As you can see, you no longer need the inner conflicts they create.

Always remember that any discomfort you are experiencing is for the purpose of gaining your attention. That all-knowing part of you is letting you know it's time to re-solve your inharmonious feelings and re-store your original harmonious feelings. Until you do this, the same old issues will continue to re-surface and plague you and create conflict. By putting your intent and motivation into action, restoring the positive, you also re-connect with the levels, layers, areas, and aspects of your Be-ing which have frozen or split off.

When you realize that changing or resolving the negative feelings is the only possible avenue for you to re-turn to your inherent feelings—your inherent nature—you will undoubtedly desire doing so. Expecting to return to your Divine nature without changing the discordant feelings is like trying to cram one more item into an already stuffed refrigerator. While restoring your inherent nature, you are also accelerating the process of re-gaining your wholeness and moving forward on your journey. You are returning to the memory of perfection in the blueprint of your DNA.

Appreciate and be grateful that another part of your inner healing is taking place every time you Script. Realize that it does not have to be something big or grandiose each time. In fact, you may have feelings that seem small and insignificant to you. Nevertheless, each Scripting is important to your wholeness.

If you have read *Feelings Buried Alive Never Die . . .* and have been using the Script, your Child, and your other aspects may have already experienced some beneficial healing. The degree of healing will, of course, be determined by the extent of Scripting and other types of effective processing you have done.

Many of us sincerely want to exhibit our better nature—our *inherent* True Self. We choose being part of the solution rather than part of the problem. Very often though, we have feelings we think are not worthy or acceptable, feelings that make us a bad person. Hence we may feel guilty for having them or ashamed of even admitting we have them. If this is the case, we usually do a very good job of trying to think away or justify these feelings. We do our best to bury the feelings or pretend they aren't even there. We may think, If I'm quiet, they might go away. Well, guess what? The feelings *don't* go away. They must be addressed and resolved.

Forgive yourself for having negative feelings and give your Self permission to let it be all right that you *do* have them. This doesn't mean you will want to keep them once you've discovered them, but you need to accept the fact that you have these feelings before you can move forward. If you keep denying that your negative feelings exist, how can they be resolved? Remember that the feelings do not make you a bad person. View yourself as a Spiritual Be-ing having a human experience, and right now you are working on your lessons.

If you find that you do have healing to accomplish, review the Script in the introduction of this book and begin processing those feelings. For assistance in identifying your feelings, there is a twenty-five page list of negative feelings with possible positive replacements beginning on page 177 of *Feelings Buried Alive Never Die* . . . .

Concentrate on processing the feelings you are still holding onto by standing in front of a mirror and looking into your eyes. Focus on your eyes as you Script until you notice a shift of energies—until you feel differently towards the people, places, circumstances, or events causing you pain or destroying your peace of mind. (Looking into your eyes in the mirror while Scripting is very effective at any time!)

After Scripting and letting go of your negative feelings toward another, you will know the extent of your healing when you think of that individual. If you experience an uncomfortable or undesirable charge of energy upon hearing the person's name or thinking about them, you will know your feelings need more processing. I suggest you again use the Script and the mirror until you know the energy between you and the other person is changed.

CHAPTER 5

Let's Get the Show on the Road

You can never fail. You just produce results.
—Dr. Wayne W. Dyer

Have you ever known anyone who seemed to continually make the right decisions and always appeared to be on the receiving end of good fortune? Did you ever wonder, How come those kinds of things don't happen to me?

Good question! Why *do* some people appear to lead a charmed life while others continually live from one crisis to the next? As you observe someone's apparently charmed life, do you ever wish you could slip into their shoes and walk the highway of their life for a while?

If so, what makes the difference? How do you come to grips with life when you recognize it is not working for you, no matter how much effort you have exerted or continue to exert in order to change it? What are the causes of the less than desirable effects? Could your choices (conscious or unconscious) be the governing factor of these effects—and of their results in your life?

You might ask, Why do I make the choices I make? Or, Why do I continue making choices that cause me to sabotage my own efforts—that end up being unproductive, that end up being big mistakes?

Mistakes? Who makes mistakes? And how do they fit in? Let's define *mistake* so we start with a common understanding. In *Noah Webster's 1828 American Dictionary of the English Language* a mistake is defined as: "To take wrong; to conceive or understand erroneously; to misunderstand or misapprehend; to error in opinion or judgment; misconception; a slip; a fault; an error."

I've met several people who don't even like to use the word *mistake*. If I don't use that word, then I won't make any, seems to be their posture. But doesn't everyone perceive or understand erroneously from time to time? Do you know anyone who never makes an error in opinion, perception, interpretation, or judgment?

Each of us has made innocent errors in judgment, perception, or understanding. None of us are perfect—we have plenty of company! When we experience an error in judgment, perception, or understanding, it's important to realize that this error in judgment leads to the choice that results in a mistake.

Regardless of early conditioning or whether our experiences are desirable or undesirable, we continually encounter the law of Cause and Effect first-hand through our choices. The effects are happening as the natural by-product of seeds planted by our choices. Accordingly, we experience the Law of the Harvest with results that are positive or not so positive.

One of the biggest challenges we face after making a mistake is preventing ourselves from feeling like complete idiots or total failures. Or we may go the other direction and have a difficult time acknowledging that we made a mistake at all. While locked into any of these feelings (idiot, failure, or inability to admit our error), the downward spiral created by our choice is prolonged. The negative effects of the choice that led to the mistake are compounded. Often, if we can't admit we've erred, we go into denial and, therefore, don't learn from our mistake. This sets us up for a repetition of the same mistake. Similarly, feeling like an idiot or a failure over a mistake also keeps us from learning. In that state we haven't the courage or self-esteem to face our error and move beyond it. By recognizing where we erred and freely acknowledging it, we begin gathering enough inner strength to pull ourselves out of that downward spiral, redirecting and correcting the course established by the mistake.

Why are errors or mistakes so prevalent? What causes our human nature to call them into existence? We have already established that mistakes come about as the natural result of any kind of inharmonious choice—our choice or another's. It would seem that we are free to choose how we feel minute to minute, to choose what we think, what we say, and what we do. We seem genuinely free to choose where we go, what we eat, and what we wear. It would seem that we are also free to choose how we act and re-act, with whom we associate, who we hire and who we fire, and on and on. But these are only true or free choices if we have been able to awaken and heal. Otherwise, these choices occur automatically and are generated out of our conditioning, whatever that may have been. In order to have mastery over our choices so that they are indeed freely made, it is essential to be awake so that our choices are no longer unconscious.

Regardless of whether our choices are free or not, they are always creating an effect—returning a consequence or result of some kind—sometimes desirable and sometimes not so desirable.

Each choice we make initiates an action or a behavior that is governed by our attitudes and beliefs. And these are dictated by our feelings and our thoughts. This is why it is so essential to consciously know what we feel and think, as this is what makes us free—free to make more harmonious, conscious, purposeful choices.

It is important to understand that your feelings (registering in your heart) and your thoughts (registering in your mind) are the forerunner to all else. When *heart* is referenced, however, that doesn't necessarily mean the heart organ. Rather, it refers to the heart of the Soul—the center or core part of you that governs your Be-ing.

Recall that your mind has to draw conclusions from the input it has been given. These conclusions determine your attitudes and beliefs, which in turn initiate or trigger your actions and behavior. All of this determines the choices you make, thereby creating the experiences you have. To reduce the above to its smallest denominator: *Your feelings and thoughts create your attitudes and beliefs, which create your actions and behavior, which create your results and reality.*

Your choices create your reality? Yes. Your choices, from the time you open your eyes in the morning until you go to sleep at night, create your reality. Some choices are innocent and inconsequential. Other choices are more significant, with far-reaching and sometimes serious ramifications.

The choices taking you in a direction that causes regret could be called incorrect or inharmonious choices, or perhaps, choices out of harmony with Universal laws—with God's laws. Further, making an inharmonious choice often propels you into a series of inharmonious choices in an effort to change unfavorable results created by your original choice. In so doing, we continue to compound and complicate the original inharmonious choice or *mis-take*.

How often do your inharmonious choices create a problem, a concern, or a negative effect for someone else? Occasionally, your choices may only affect your *Self*, but as a rule, each inharmonious choice carries with it definite reverberations that influence many.

When any of us experience hurt, pain, unkind words, or shameful acts, it is the result of someone's incorrect choice—someone's mistaken use of free will—that usually robs another of their free will. The choice becomes incorrect the moment an adverse effect is set into motion. Regardless of whose choice is responsible for initiating the adverse effect in us, our human nature is to passionately protect our Be-ing from further hurt and pain. When we feel threatened because of someone else's choice, our survival machinery automatically goes into the "fight or flight" mode. If we tend toward "flight" and become defensive or afraid—as is most often the case during childhood (or even later if our self-esteem has suffered)—we respond by adding one more block to our wall, thereby shielding our *Self* from any additional assaults. Bit by bit, as each block is placed, a part of our Be-ing automatically withdraws; and we become further detached and separated from humankind. In time, our wall can become so wide and so high that our feelings are shut off entirely. It just hurts too much to feel. As a result, we lose touch with others and find ourselves more and more removed, isolated, and alone. We also become detached from the world. Our sensibilities slowly glaze over, become numb and may eventually turn off. At this juncture, we become dis-connected, not only from others, but from our *Self.* This condition occurs unconsciously as a result of being human and alive.

At one of my workshops, Jane, a woman in her early 40's had unknowingly created a very high and impenetrable wall around herself. Her feelings were numbed. During the seminar Jane participated in an experiential process to get in touch with feelings she'd experienced in her family dynamics as a youth. Her participation in this activity awakened many old hurts and feelings which had been disconnected, buried and forgotten. When Jane realized what had unconsciously happened to her, she was truly grateful for the opportunity to re-discover her buried feelings. During this process, Jane came to understand that unless she discovered what her blocked feelings were, she would never be able to resolve and heal them.

Jane had not recognized how she had separated herself from her father through the resentment she felt toward him. Nor had she realized that she had unconsciously hidden inside herself. As she began to understand the role she had unknowingly accepted as a child, Jane sadly discovered that she had numerous feelings to heal where her father was concerned. After the workshops, armed with the desire to change her negative feelings toward him, she Scripted for a period of time to re-frame the view of him which had originated in her childhood perceptions. By Scripting, Jane was

able to re-establish tender feelings for her father and to forgive him from her heart.

A few months after she had done this, Jane's mother and
father, who lived in a neighboring state, came to spend a
few days with her. She was not prepared for the wonderful
difference she felt in her father's presence. Jane was finally
able to carry on a conversation with him without feeling
anxiety. It was almost as if they were discovering each other
for the first time! Jane felt she had found a new friend. She
was so thrilled at the beautiful change taking place in their
relationship! For the first time in her life she wished their
visit could have been prolonged. Tears of sincere caring,
love, and joy were shed as Jane's parents departed. She truly
did not want their visit to come to an end.

Sadly, Jane could not have been prepared for the tragic
news she received before the end of that day. On their trip
home, Jane's father passed away while he was napping.
What a shock! But oh, how very, very grateful Jane was that
she had healed her feelings towards her father before he
passed on.

We never know what may happen, do we? Isn't it sad
that we let opportunities pass us by when we could say a
kind word, give encouragement, reassure someone, or let a
loved one know of our love and caring for them?

What is it about human nature that makes it so challenging to face and resolve our less than glorious feelings
toward others? How can we overcome this tendency? Is it
possible to re-solve our feelings and forgive the ones we've
held responsible for our pain?

When we harbor feelings against someone, we create a
sense of separateness, of dis-connectedness. And no matter

what the feelings are, they're usually due to our incorrect perceptions, something missed in understanding—mis-understanding. We experience mental confusion and per-haps feel lost. We find ourselves out there searching for something, but we don't know what that something is.

Although conditions occur in our lives for which we are not responsible (our negative feelings may seem to be caused by outside forces), we are the only ones capable of healing them. There are "tools" (some presented in this book) that have the capacity to help us resolve them. We *can* choose.

As you recall, the wall being erected by our underlying feelings has been under construction throughout our life. When did its construction start? At some point, this wall began inhibiting our progress and hampering our ability to move forward in discovering our Truth. As our wall grew wider and higher, we unknowingly became a prisoner within the very confines being erected for our protection.

With each negative feeling, thought, attitude, word, and action; with our inability to resolve our inner turmoil or confusion, our wall continues to grow until we discover its existence and effect its dismantling.

If we are not aware of this wall, achieving inner peace may take much longer than necessary, as it did with Jane and her father. Once we recognize and own the fact that we may have a wall, bringing it down becomes our greatest desire, for this wall covers a very significant door, a door we subconsciously yearn to open and enter. Inside the door is our most rare treasure.

Consequently, being liberated from our own prison and placing ourself at the threshold of our unique door is the intrinsic desire of each of us. Only by cultivating awareness will our natural motivation shift us into a higher gear and provide the energy required to accomplish our liberation. For when we walk through this door, we reconnect with the person for whom we have been searching all of our life— our True Self! Our Divine Self! The Love that we are.

By reuniting with the Truth of your Be-ing, you re-establish the alignment that offers the comfort and peace for which you may be longing, the love and acceptance for which you may be craving, the joy and happiness for which you may desperately be yearning, and the compassion you may sadly be lacking because you have forgotten how to *feel*. As you reclaim your glorious qualities, you allow your *Self* to heal your feelings from *inside your heart*—from the inside–out.

Those evasive, beautiful attributes deep inside your Soul have been waiting for an invitation to re-appear—to re-join you. They respond and rejoice when they are uncovered and rediscovered—when they are once again recognized as an integral and important part of your *Self*. (Remember, the tools in this book assist you in accomplishing these goals).

By resolving any hurt, pain, unkind words or shameful acts and their resultant feelings, you are clearing up long-standing, unfinished business. And when you choose to do this willingly, letting go of the "you should" pattern, you are also exercising your God-given power of choice, thus reclaiming your Will. You are acting from *your* Will (and God's Will), not someone else's will, which is indeed crucial in bringing down your wall and enjoying true freedom.

At this point you could be standing at your door! Will you contemplate opening it and re-connecting with the

Truth of your Be-ing? Will you re-claim your intrinsic gifts of freedom, comfort and peace, unconditional love, absolute joy, happiness, and contentment? Or are you comfortable with the status quo? If you are, the wall will stay there and the door will remain closed. It is true that you will be absolving yourself of any need to look further, but it may come at a very high price.

Consider something that my friend, Lutie Larsen, came to understand: "Until you recognize and decide to do something about your issues (feelings), you only live a *portion* of your life!" And, I might add, you never allow yourself the golden opportunity of knowing your True Self, thereby missing one of the most monumental and magnificent discoveries in the world! If you could only see your own magnificence, you would be in total awe!

CHAPTER 6

Stripping Away

When we make a mistake, Jesus doesn't say,
"Go to your room!" He says, "Come unto me."

—Dr. Wayne W. Dyer

For those of us having a challenge moving into our magnificence, perhaps examining our unknown erroneous beliefs will be helpful.

Have you ever known anyone who made a mistake? Was it considered a sin? Could it be possible there are people who believe this? Frequently, because sin is such a ponderous topic, we don't care to be reminded of its reality. It is even difficult to admit we may have committed sin. Why?

Is it because we weary of the blame and shame game? Does the subject dredge up feelings we'd rather keep buried? Is it because the word *sin* elicits feelings of guilt within the *Self*? Are we afraid of a justice which lacks compassion and mercy from others?—from God? Do we lose hope when we recognize our sins—when we realize how many poor choices we have made? For many of us, we'd rather ignore the entire discussion of sin.

Most of my life I genuinely disliked the word *sin*. It held such negative connotations for me. "Surely, sin has nothing to do with me!" I thought. I reasoned that if I obeyed the "Thou Shalt's" and "Thou Shalt Not's" I would be reasonably safe. My perception was that the real sinners were murderers, robbers, liars, dishonest people, and the like.

Still, it bothered me greatly when I learned that the Bible (Romans 3:23) refers to us all as sinners. Webster's definition didn't help either: "Someone who violates a moral or divine law; any voluntary transgression of religious laws or moral principles; a breach."

Perhaps pride had kept me from exploring my *Self*, from understanding how I truly stood in this regard. I came to realize that there was much more to sin than I had allowed in my narrow definition.

Then, much to my joy, just a few years ago I learned that the Hebrew definition of *sin* is: "missing the mark" or "missing the point." "Missing the mark," I thought—of course! Such a simple definition for such an important concept. Doesn't each of us *miss the mark* every day in some regard? (I'll let you determine the meaning of the mark.)

Shortly after learning this new definition, someone shared with me the acronym for sin—**S**elf **I**mposed **N**onsense. Yes. How appropriate and how true it is. We do create a lot of nonsense in our lives.

What a heavy burden these new awarenesses lifted from me! I had to ask myself, "Does anyone stay on course in every regard all the time?" The answer didn't excuse me from missing the mark or imposing nonsense on myself, but it did grant me permission to quit feeling guilty and being so hard on myself.

I came to understand that I don't have to be absolutely perfect before I leave this world! Yes, I can allow myself weaknesses and imperfections that, with time and correct choices, I will be able to surmount. Now I understand that hitting the mark is a process of changing, of stripping away, of letting go of all that is less than glorious.

But what's wrong with missing the mark? you may ask. The significance of missing the mark is the cumulative influence it brings to your inner *Self*—to your essence, to your very Soul. Each time you miss the mark you get off course; you relinquish a degree of contentment and peace; you unknowingly lose sight of your True Self—of your Soul Pattern. You may find your *Self* compromising, thus creating energy constrictions—binding, contracting, compressing—in your Be-ing. And when your energy flow is constricted you automatically choke your progress.

Missing the mark creates subtle dis-harmonies which breed separateness and chaos in your life, pulling you down in all areas of your *Soul.* You add more protective blocks to your wall, thereby making it higher and higher—all of which begins to isolate you, not only from others, but from your Maker. Your False *Self* comes to the forefront. Your light becomes weaker and more obscured, thus, continuing to distance you from your real Source.

As all of this is happening you accept the role of "actor" rather than purposely choosing that of "author" in which you consciously write your life's drama. While Be-ing the actor you take directions from anyone and everyone—except your Maker. Whereas, when you become the author you make choices which bring you back into harmony and your true course. Yes—*you* choose your course.

But isn't it all right for me to make a mistake, to make an undesirable or unwise choice, to miss the mark?

Sure it is! What's important is to *own* your mistakes—not deny them. By owning the choices you have made, you allow your mistakes to become stepping stones in your unique learning experiences, which is why you are here in the first place. You are here to learn by *feeling* your experiences, by coming to recognize what is harmonious and what is inharmonious for you—what is wise and what is unwise.

Sometimes the only way we learn is by suffering the effects of our inharmonious or unwise choices—by making mistakes and truly experiencing the feelings these mistakes bring to us.

The sooner we recognize and acknowledge the feelings we have when we do make an unwise or undesirable choice—when we miss the mark—the faster we can reverse the negative effect our choice is creating. We can re-route and correct the direction of the undesirable choice. It's like finding ourselves doing a nose-dive in an airplane but pulling out of that nose-dive before it's too late.

Occasionally someone we know and trust may discern a pattern of inharmonious choices in us and is kind enough to bring it to our attention. Suggestions offered from another's view point may provide helpful insights for us. Perhaps they are seeing and perceiving from a different vantage point and understand something we don't. Their desire may be to help reduce the suffering we seem to continually experience by repeating unproductive patterns. If we give ourselves permission to acknowledge that we could perhaps learn from their recommendations, we may find this an opportunity to grow emotionally. We can also be grateful the well-meaning person cares enough to point out these weaknesses.

If you find that someone's suggestion really bothers you, it might serve to go deep inside and ask your *Self* how much your ego is vested in being right (in control). Difficulty granting yourself permission to be wrong may indicate you have some introspection and processing to do. You might begin by Scripting for the feelings that someone's suggestions have brought into focus. Allow your mature, adult *Self* to accept someone's observation. You may wish to tell them, "Thank you for sharing," and then let it go; or you may feel inclined to discuss it.

An important caution, however, is to acknowledge and trust your intuitive sense to know if someone is interfering rather than being concerned for your welfare. Sometimes it may be hard to distinguish ego feelings from those of a legitimate response to someone violating your boundaries. Usually, if the ego is in charge, you will find yourself over-reacting and your response will be out of proportion to what has been said.

If someone's suggestion really "bugs" you (such as when you feel they have interfered in your business or attacked you), *Script* that feeling until you can allow the feeling without having an emotional response to it. Then, be willing to look inward and consider implementing what they suggest, if the suggestion is viable.

Recognize that others cannot write your life script for you. Whether their suggestions are valid or not so valid, you must create the script which enables your true *Self*—and its attendant harmony—to thrive. Gaining confidence in one's intuition also comes from praying diligently, listening to your inner voice, learning, and seeking wise counsel. If you ask a question long enough, you *will* receive the answer. It may come in a most unusual way, but it will come.

Let us now re-visit the concept of ego. Ego is Latin for Self. In counseling circles, the ego is associated with self-ish-ness, with immediate gratification.

If we reject well-intentioned advice from others or dis-trust our own intuitions, the indication is that we are stuck in areas or aspects of our Be-ing. Or, it could indicate a lack of awareness and that we are not ready for the truth about our *Self*. If we are stuck, energy flow is constricted and we experience faceless pain. The ego or False Self goes into overdrive attempting to control us. When the ego is in the driver's seat, our False Self, rather than our True Self, has taken charge and is the one experiencing the negative feel-ings.

The question may come to mind, How do I know if I lack awareness? The answer is that you know by your own suffering and the suffering your behavior has caused, or continues to cause, others. When there is suffering, it is a sure indication that emotional and spiritual growth are vital needs at this time in our lives.

Another question that may arise is, How do we know when the False Self is in charge? We can recognize the False Self by our feelings of shame, blame, guilt, put-down, and worthlessness. Or, by the False Self's tendency to be self-seeking and self-absorbed, and its desire for adulation and self-glory. Another clue that helps us know the False Self is in charge is when we need to be right all the time. If any of these qualities are present, they are impeding emotional and spiritual growth. We cannot be our True Self, because our

True Self is only Love.

Glenda Green shares with us in her book, *Love Without End:*

> The love that you are is your real self-glory. Consequently, your knowledge of true self is being destroyed by the dominance of ego. . . . *Ego* is composed of all the fictions we have used to replace the love that we are. Creating an ego is the greatest sacrifice we have ever made. . . . Remember, the ego is the personal fiction that attempts to subvert and replace the love that you are. . . . In contrast with love, the ego feeds upon fear and is driven by all the mechanisms of fear.

In other words, the negative feelings expressed by the False Self stem from fears lodged in our ego. These fears cause us to over-react. When beset by fear and insecurity our ego seizes power, and in a zealous effort to protect our *Self,* starts running the show. The ego believes that our survival depends on it "taking over." An overbearing, over-protective ego, like an over-protective parent, keeps us from experiencing our own self-reliance and hinders us in the establishment of a healthy sense of self-worth.

A good way to determine if the ego is in charge is by monitoring our feelings. Feelings are offended *only* when ego is vested in the outcome—when ego is out of balance, when it needs to be in charge. Sometimes, however, the offense or hurt may come due to a very tender and uncertain ego. Nonetheless, the ego is still in control.

If our ego doesn't allow for admitting that we may be wrong—that we could use some changing—we are probably experiencing a difficult time moving forward. If this is the case, the False Self needs to get out of the way!

At this point, let's talk about pride. As with most words, *pride* has many definitions, both positive and negative. According to Noah Webster, the adverse attributes of pride, include inordinate self-esteem; an unreasonable conceit of one's own superiority in talents, beauty, wealth, accomplishments, rank of elevation in office, which manifests itself in lofty airs, distance, reserve, and often in contempt of others; insolence; rude treatment of others; insolent exultation; that of which men are proud; that which excites boasting.

Pride is essentially competitive in nature. Feelings of adverse pride are an indication that the ego is struggling for control. According to C. S. Lewis

> Pride gets no pleasure out of having something, only out of having more of it than the next man—it is the comparison that makes you proud. The pleasure of being above the rest. Once the element of competition has gone, pride has gone.

All of these attributes of pride are elements of missing the mark, but the heart or core of pride remains unspoken. The central feature of pride is enmity—enmity toward God and enmity toward our fellow man. (Enmity means hatred toward, hostility to, or a state of opposition toward).

Webster defines the more welcome attributes of pride as: "Generous elation of heart; a noble self-esteem springing from a consciousness of worth; decoration; ornament; beauty displayed; splendid show; to value oneself; to gratify self-esteem."

Sometimes we have a difficult time distinguishing between inordinate pride and a healthy self-esteem. There is a fine line between the two. This is the main reason for being alert and in touch with our feelings and thoughts. You will generally find that people with healthy self-esteem have no need to find fault, to gossip, or to backbite. They don't envy or covet nor are they jealous. A balanced sense of one's worth fosters selflessness, humility, forgiveness, peace, acceptance, gratitude, genuineness, and the ability to praise or lift others.

Healthy self-esteem is refreshing, exhilarating and exciting! People with this esteem are usually genuine and caring. We feel comfortable in their presence and enjoy being around them. There usually is no pretense nor need to prove or put on airs. There is no "mask" with those of noble self-esteem. As you incorporate these favorable characteristics, you can honestly say you are beginning to live life to its fullest.

These positive attributes are not present when one's actions come from undue pride, lofty airs, emotional distance or reserve, or contempt for others. Negative qualities of pride are usually an overcompensation for feelings of insecurity and fear. They are the ego's attempt to make the individual feel adequate and safe. Ultimately, however, they disable the individual by keeping him/her from experiencing who they are.

A prideful individual has forgotten that real security resides in knowing that, ultimately, God is the one in charge. And because pride is essentially competitive in nature, we sometimes pit our will (perspective, authority, knowledge, abilities, opinions) against God's. We set up the dynamic of "My will" rather than "Thy will" be done.

A prideful person has forgotten the saying, Let go and

let God. Have you heard the acronym for *EGO*—**E**dging **G**od **O**ut? When we Edge God Out, we choose to be on our own. At that point, it's impossible for Him to assist us.

As a friend of mine recently observed, A healthy self-regard is the best protection against an over-blown sense of pride. When we recognize our own self-worth, we have no need to fear comparison or to overcompensate for any sense of inadequacy—we won't *have* a sense of inadequacy!

By letting go of the false security of pride and embracing the true security of our connection to Love—to God—we can recognize our own worth. We are able to let go of negative pride when we honestly look within, with a sincere desire to rid ourselves of dis-harmony.

Until pride is eliminated we have a difficult time being teachable; we expect the other person to make amends first; we have a hard time asking someone to forgive us. Admitting we have made a mistake or that we are wrong is difficult, as is owning responsibility for our life's choices and experiences. Sadly, even using the word pride or proud can thrust us into an egotistical, haughty, self-serving attitude, one that further distances us from genuine self-esteem.

But what about righteous pride? Is there such a thing as being righteously proud? Perhaps the answer is in how one measures righteousness.

We would do well to look at some of our uses of the word proud. Instead of being proud, how would it feel being *honored* or *pleased* or *privileged*? In the case of our children, how would it be to let them know we sincerely enjoy their success. By applying these words we are teaching them a beautiful and beneficial way of valuing human worth.

I finally understood this spiritual principle after learning it from a wonderful teacher. I will never forget the feeling that flooded over me when I first replaced proud with another word.

My younger son, then 21, had just done something which truly exhibited to me the fine young man that he is. He was sitting by me on the couch, leaning forward, at the time. I automatically put my arm around him and said, "I'm so"—and I started to say "*proud*" but quickly caught myself—"I'm so *honored* to be your mother." I cannot describe the feeling those words elicited in me! I felt such a reverence for his life and a new depth of appreciation for the blessing and privilege of being his mother.

Think about commending someone you love. Even though you may want to use the word "proud," consider using honored or privileged in its place. Experience the feeling.

My elder son is well known in Country Music circles. (He's a songwriter and the keyboard player in "Diamond Rio"). Consequently, people are always congratulating my husband and me on Dan's success, usually with the words, "I'll bet you're sure proud of him." I truly understand that everyone is sincere and means well, and I genuinely appreciate their interest and support. Nonetheless, hearing the word *proud* in this regard now causes me uneasiness. My response is always, "We're very *pleased* he's realizing his dreams and having such wonderful experiences."

By eliminating pride of *Self* and becoming more cognizant of how we use these words, we experience life from a whole different perspective—one that is unfamiliar to most of us. The competitive spirit disappears. We stop being concerned about others getting ahead of us, or of being jealous or envious of others. Worrying about those around us having more or being more is no longer a reason to fear. Our demeanor changes. We can easily laugh at our own mistakes. Letting go of old resentments and hurts—forgiving others—is much easier. We are more open to loving and being loved. We feel sincerely happy for another's accomplishments and successes.

We can sit back and delight in watching others enjoy the limelight without feeling slighted or threatened. Someone else can receive the credit for something we initiated or contributed to and it doesn't make any difference. If we're overlooked, it's okay; we don't have to smolder inside or dwell on it. We can let it go.

In the final analysis, by eliminating words, attitudes, and patterns of pride, we are letting go of the need to be better than others. We aren't driven to prove our worth and our place in society. Letting go creates more room in our heart for amplifying the *Love* that we are—love for *Self* and love for others.

So how do you get to this point? Ann Brewer, author of *The Power of Twelve* and recognized expert on the inner workings of DNA, submits that by *Scripting* a particular feeling for 21 successive days, a re-patterned DNA may result. In other words, the emotional imprint in your DNA, which has accumulated and impacted you throughout life, can be changed.

The feelings of inordinate pride can be replaced. If you find, however, that your behavior pattern takes a little longer to change, continue Scripting until any undesirable pride or its appendages have been eliminated from your attitudes, words, and behavior. Who knows? There may be a very large deposit of pride in your family's DNA. It didn't get there overnight so it might not disappear overnight! Be willing to give it time and consistent effort. The rewards will greatly outweigh the effort.

Now let us address another face of pride. This one is just as deleterious to our emotional and spiritual growth as haughtiness. Life always gives us polarities, so in this connection I refer to those who lack self-esteem or *Self*-definition. The challenges these individuals experience aren't as evident, perhaps, as another person's. Nonetheless, they are just as painful and difficult to resolve. There are answers for those who may find themselves in this arena. (These answers are discussed at length in Chapter 19, "Revere Your Self.")

So walk with me, if you will, through these next chapters to gain the insights necessary to prepare for revering your *Self.*

We have talked about our mis-takes (or could we call them illnesses, experiences, and challenges?) and how they can lead us in many different directions—all of them detours from our main road. We unconsciously create these detours through innocent, inappropriate choices.

Perhaps with a bit of introspection we might question whether our choices were *indeed* inappropriate. For if we hadn't made a particular choice at a particular time, we might not have gained the experience necessary for our growth. So, were they really mistakes?

Look at the bright side of your seemingly erroneous choice—the mistake, the experience, the challenge—and ask yourself: What am I learning from this experience? What is it teaching me? What is it about me that I'm not in touch with? What do I need to know that I didn't know before?

Honestly evaluate each learning opportunity with which you have gifted yourself. Even though you may not enjoy the experience while it's happening, open your eyes wide and look—really look. Perhaps you will be able to see what you are doing to your *Self.* But don't just look—SEE it! FEEL it!

Allow yourself to be taught by each experience! Pray for an understanding of it! Readily accept the lesson, the message, whatever it is. Let it be all right if you didn't score on this one, if your common sense didn't serve you so well, if you didn't come out on top. It really doesn't matter, just as long as you are learning and growing from your experience—from your choice. Nor does it matter what others might think of you. It's okay! It's *your* journey! Just regard it as one more stepping stone in your life.

If it is difficult to be objective at the time you are going through a learning experience, realize that eventually you *will* be able to understand the benefit you received from it. Quit beating yourself over the head. Let go of the guilt. Forgive yourself. Move on with joy and gratitude for the learning experience! It has given you added wisdom and is preparing you for something of which you know not.

By doing so, you will find that extracting understanding and wisdom from your experiences becomes easier each time. Your evaluation can now be placed in your mental files. If and when you do need it for future reference, you can readily pull it up and use it to make wiser choices. With each learning experience you will find that your awareness sharpens. It will become easier to recognize and prevent recurring energy-draining patterns—the ones that could head you in the same old unproductive directions.

I'm reminded of a young man who seems to have a penchant for creating crisis after crisis in his life. If this pattern happens to have a break in it, where he's not dealing with a crisis, he unknowingly and automatically sets one into motion.

Individuals in his immediate and extended family never know when they might be the central figure in one of these crises. It's as if he doesn't know how to function without a crisis taking place in his life. The interesting thing is, each crisis is always someone else's fault, in his mind, and the whole world seems to be against him. Observing this pattern in the young man's life has been most interesting, and a real schooling for friends and family who understand what is taking place.

Along with needing to experience a crisis, this same young man also appears to thrive on having an enemy or two at any given moment—someone he's at odds with. While going through the enemy phenomena, he won't speak to them if he's in their presence. In fact, he acts as if they're not even there. If another person enters the picture who can be his enemy, all of a sudden, the first one is no longer an enemy. He talks with them and treats them as if there was never anything wrong—like they're old friends.

How important is it to recognize crippling patterns in our own lives? Can we prepare our children for making responsible choices so they will avoid establishing unhealthy patterns? Step by step we can provide opportunities which call for simple choices while our children are young. By allowing them to experience the natural consequences of their choices through the years, without us interceding, making wise decisions will become a matter of course for them.

How will they learn if we constantly intercede? Each time we rescue them from a dilemma—not allowing them to feel the natural consequences of their own actions—we are contributing (however subtly) to the development of an irresponsible human being. Ultimately we are putting ourselves in their debt. How? By robbing them of their learning experiences. You see, they will have to repeat similar experiences until they learn what they need to learn. We literally cripple them by not allowing the growth that evolves from natural consequences. As a result, we deny them opportunities to become responsible human Be-ings.

This doesn't mean we can't support them in their learning. Nor does it mean we have to pound guilt into them. They usually feel guilty or sorrowful enough without our reminding them. We can still love and accept them unconditionally. The Lord continues loving us when we make mistakes. Remember, Jesus doesn't say, "Go to your room." He says, "Come unto me."

As parents, we can lovingly and calmly counsel our children. We can help them see where their choices took them, or where they might take them—without implying what we feel they should do. They will learn without our implications throwing them into shame. Then when future decisions need to be made, we can lovingly point out the possible outcome of each of their choices so they are better prepared to understand the alternatives. Keep in mind, there comes a time—who knows the age?—when a child does not like to be told what to do anymore than we do.

(Nevertheless, at times it may be imperative to let them know what is best for them.)

We can also counsel them to ask themselves: Will the choice I am considering bring the results I am seeking? Will it assist me in moving forward on my journey? Will it keep me out of harm's way?

Whatever we do as parents, we must: Love, Love, Love. Accept, Accept, Accept. Support, Support, Support. Allow, Allow, Allow the natural consequences!

By making harmonious choices—as parents and children—we automatically reap the benefits of observing universal laws. If your approach to life is not producing the desired harvest, perhaps it's time to examine that approach and consider putting a process into action for changing it.

Have you heard the saying, If you always do what you've always done, you'll always get what you always got? By repeating the same kinds of mistakes over and over again, eventually it pains us in some area of our life so much that we may finally recognize its wake up call. By not getting the message or learning the lesson the first, second, or third time, we find ourselves duplicating the situation, the pattern, the pain, until we do get the message—until we ultimately understand.

Did you know that Abraham Lincoln failed in business twice before the age of 25? That he had a nervous breakdown at age 27? That he was defeated for Speaker, for Elector, and for Congress before he was finally elected to Congress at age 37? Did you know that two years later he was once again defeated for Congress, then defeated for the Senate, and for Vice President, then defeated for the Senate again? Yes, he was defeated in elections a total of eight times before being elected President of the United States. Do you think he learned anything or gained any wisdom during all of those defeats? Do you think he made any changes in his life because of those defeats? Did he have tenacity? How many people would stay the course the way he did?

Perhaps Lincoln's example teaches us that each mistake or each loss can be a stepping stone to new understanding. Making an inharmonious choice or a mistake is not the problem, for doing so doesn't make us less of a person or suggest that we are failing. A person only fails by giving up. It's whether we are learning from that mistake, how we are handling it, and if we are achieving productive growth because of it.

You're on the road to success when you realize that failure is only a detour. I don't know who said that, but isn't it interesting? Here's another: A man may fail many times, but he isn't a failure until he begins to blame somebody else. I wonder if Abraham Lincoln blamed anyone else for his seeming failures.

Don't we all make mistakes—incorrect choices—from time to time? Don't we all miss the mark? If we aren't enjoying the results of our mistakes, are we motivated to change our feelings and thoughts, as well as our attitudes and behavior? Isn't it true, most generally, that we only pause and look within (assuming we are willing to take responsibility) when something goes wrong?

Why do we avoid ourselves so strenuously? Is it because we're afraid of what we might find? Could avoidance possibly be why so many people are in perpetual motion, constantly going places, keeping themselves busy; or always needing to have the television or radio playing? How often do we stop our world and go "within?" How often do we actually take inventory of what's in our heart?

Remember, when you acknowledge the truth in your heart—of anything in life that isn't working for you, or any undesirable characteristic—it sets you free. It's only by admitting the truth in your heart, and letting it be all right, that you really begin moving forward.

By examining, allowing, and then applying your new awarenesses you free yourself of unproductive living. Yes, application is necessary. Commitment is also necessary. Having an intellectual understanding of these principles but not applying them doesn't get the job done! In order to create the desired change in your life, commitment to applying correct principles is imperative. You will not experience change if, after trying it a few times, something doesn't work and you just dismiss it with, "Oh, well . . . ." Change usually takes on-going effort.

Give your *Self* permission to claim the benefits that come from resolving your inharmonious feelings, thoughts, attitudes, and beliefs. You no longer need attributes that govern undesirable choices with resultant, lose-lose outcomes.

While you are in the process of generating an internal shift, choices or decisions similar to the ones you have made in the past may once again face you. With a new awareness of how feelings impact your life's experiences, you are now better prepared to make wiser and more appropriate choices. These choices can now keep you from repeating the same unproductive patterns. Knowing what to watch for gives you a greater sense of focus. Your direction becomes clearer as you re-position your *Self* on your designated road. You have the opportunity of becoming the author of your life, of putting your *Self* in charge. As this takes place, you have more sense of your inner strength and power—the power God bestowed upon you when you came here.

Could it be that we are here learning to recognize and discover our True Self through our experiences? Have we indeed chosen our own set of circumstances (as people who have had near-death experiences tell us) to learn and re-discover the truth of our *Selves*? What better vehicle of checks and balances are there than undergoing experiences which prompt us to look within for answers?

In the book, *Embraced by the Light*, Betty Eadie shares with us a portion of her near-death experience which illustrates this point.

> Coming to earth is much like selecting a college and choosing a course of study. We are all at various levels of spiritual development, and we have come here in the stations that best suit our spiritual needs. The minute we judge others for their faults or shortcomings, we are displaying similar shortcomings in ourselves. We don't have the knowledge to judge people accurately here.
>
> As if to illustrate this principle for me, the heavens scrolled back, and I saw the earth again. This time my vision focused on a street corner in a large city. There, I saw a man lying in a drunken stupor on the sidewalk near a building. One of my guides said, "What do you see?"
>
> "Why, a drunken bum lying in his wallow," I said, not understanding why I had to see this. My guides became excited. They said, "Now we will show you who he really is."
>
> His spirit was revealed to me, and I saw a magnificent

man, full of light. Love emanated from his being, and I understood that he was greatly admired in the heavens. This great being came to earth as a teacher to help a friend that he had spiritually bonded with.

His friend was a prominent attorney who had an office a few blocks away from this corner. Although the drunk now had no recollection of this agreement with his friend, his purpose was to be a reminder to him of the needs of others. I understood that the attorney was naturally compassionate, but seeing the drunk would spark him to do more for those who needed his means.

I knew that they would see each other, and the attorney would recognize the spirit within the drunk—the man within the man—and be moved to do much good. They would never know their covenanted roles here, but their missions would be fulfilled nonetheless. The drunk had sacrificed his time on earth for the benefit of another. His development would continue and other things he might need for progression would be given him later.

"Sometimes a noble failure serves the world as faithfully as a distinguished success." —Anonymous

None of us has pure knowledge. How can we judge another correctly? We haven't walked in their moccasins. We weren't there when they experienced the treatment or conditions that caused the behavior they exhibit.

As we embrace this truth, how can we fault the people who are responsible (as we see it) for the malice we hold in our hearts and bodies against them? These people are in our lives for a reason. These people are our teachers. They are here to deliver a lesson. Let us rejoice in the effectiveness of their teaching!

There's an old saying: No man is your enemy, no man is your friend, every man is your teacher. In fact, every person, place, circumstance, and event with which you are involved is either your teacher or part of your lesson plan. How you deal with them is, perhaps, a major portion of your study— of your test. Each one assists you in your *re-search*.

CHAPTER 7

What Am I Learning?

Change starts when someone sees the next step.

—William Drayton

Let us say that everything that occurs in our lives happens for a reason. Let us also suppose that everyone understands and accepts this premise as true. How would it be if each person started asking, Why am I having this experience? What am I learning from this experience? What is it mirroring to me about myself? Imagine if each individual looked inward instead of outward for the cause of the undesirable things happening in their life!

You have undoubtedly heard it said that you create your own reality. Have you ever wondered just what this means? To understand this concept, we must recognize that everything is created spiritually before it is created physically. For example, great symphonies are heard before they are scored; great structures are envisioned before the architect puts pen to paper.

But how are things created spiritually? *Everything* is created through *subtle energies*—energies on the molecular level. You can't see them with your physical eyes, hear them with your physical ears, or feel them with your physical touch.

What is this subtle energy? Where does it come from?

Subtle energies are vibrational frequencies created in the spiritual energy field before they take a physical form. For the purposes of this book, our feelings and thoughts are our spiritual creations wherein energies are born and eventually move into the physical. Even though there are countless subtle energies (positive, negative and neutral) in our universe, we are concerned with the subtle energies our feelings and thoughts create. Each feeling and each thought generates a particular energy. Physicists tell us that our thoughts create literal "thought fields" This same principle holds true for our feelings—they create "feeling fields."

It's important to keep in mind that our thoughts are governed by our feelings. The more intense our feelings and thoughts are (in any area of our life), the more energy we are giving to the creation of a particular energy field. Yes, that upon which our feelings and thoughts focus creates ever more pronounced energy fields.

Whether we concentrate on the positive or the negative, we still create. We are always creating. Positive intention keeps us in harmony with the Love that we are; negative intention contaminates our spiritual, emotional, mental, and physical fields. Extensive research has revealed that negative energy actually harms biological tissue. The dis-harmony resulting from the negative we focus upon jams our spiritual guidance system.

Accordingly, you may feel as did Job of old: "For the thing which I greatly feared is come upon me, and that which I was afraid of is come unto me" (Job 3:25). The antidote, we learn, is love. Consider John's counsel: "There is no fear in love; but perfect love casteth out fear: because fear hath torment. He that feareth is not made perfect in love" (1 John 4:18).

By giving your energy to loving and trusting God, your *Self,* and others (and knowing that your desired results are being accomplished), your reality can be much more peaceful, productive and freeing. All in all, what you experience as your reality is born of the subtle energies of your feelings and thoughts.

Granted, those who have had limited opportunities to make choices as children, and have been conditioned to react, are disadvantaged. Consequently, even thinking or speaking for the *Self* can be frightening, unnatural, unnerving. Nevertheless, you still experience the results of your emotions—your feelings and thoughts. Therefore, a lot of inner healing may be necessary before you are prepared to change the direction of your life.

Each one of us will eventually realize whom we may look to when we desire change in our life. We may require extensive therapy before we reach the point of being able to work through everyday challenges alone. But when we are finally able to shed the role of victim, a whole new world opens up to us.

In the final analysis, who do you turn to to "fix" your reality? One of the most powerful and consequential lessons to learn in this life is that *only **you** can fix your own reality, your own world.* Because you have created it, albeit unknowingly, only you can un-create it. This cannot be accomplished with drugs, liquor, food, or other escape routes. These things only mask the symptoms; they don't resolve them. The change must be accomplished from the inside out, rather than from the outside in.

Each of us is here facing the same kinds of challenges, wading through the same swamp, dodging the same alligators, looking for the same answers, and striving to reach the same destination. Each person simply reaches their moment of truth at a different time, in a different way, and in a different body.

By truly understanding and internalizing the principle that only *we* can fix our own world, we create a shift of major proportions. The shift comes both in our feeling nature and in the way we view and approach life. This consciousness shift can bring about an effortless surrender of judging and blaming others for the conditions in which we find ourselves. Whoever we have been blaming did not create our challenges (although they may have contributed to them). They can not fix them. Only we can! Only we can decide whether the glass is half full or half empty. Only we can determine whether our reality becomes a triumph or a tragedy.

An amazing story of a tragedy turned triumph is that of Amy Biehl. Amy was a young American dedicated to working with blacks in South Africa to improve the ghettos of Cape Town. During the last turbulent weeks of apartheid, when blacks took to the streets in violent protest, she was stabbed and beaten to death by four young men caught up in the rioting. She was killed for no reason other than being white—the color of the oppressors—and being in the wrong place at the wrong time.

Amy's story is one of four that appear in an award-winning documentary, *Long Night's Journey into Day*, filmed during hearings of South Africa's Truth and Reconciliation Commission. The TRC was proposed by Bishop Desmond

Tutu to help the country move beyond its violent past and heal the deep wounds inflicted during apartheid and its downfall. With a goal of restorative rather than retributive justice, the commission grants amnesty to political criminals, both black and white, in exchange for "full disclosure"—in exchange for *Truth*.

After three years of imprisonment, Amy's murderers petitioned the TRC for amnesty. When Amy's parents heard this, they made a remarkable decision. Although still grieving for their daughter, they chose to go to South Africa to visit the neighborhood where Amy's killers had lived, to meet their families, and most remarkable of all, to testify at the TRC in support of amnesty for the young men.

In a moving scene from the documentary, they explain that their decision was to honor their daughter and her beliefs. Amy had worked hard and won the hearts of many of the people she was helping. She had also indelibly established her value in their lives. Her parents felt strongly that Amy, had she been there, would have supported amnesty. The respect they showed for their daughter and her cause, whatever they themselves may have believed, and their capacity to forgive those who had caused them so much pain, was an eye-opener to all involved. Even the families of the young men responsible for Amy's death were amazed.

At the hearings, the young men listened with somber expressions as the Biehls told of Amy's work and commitment. They told of a letter she had written to a Cape Town newspaper just weeks before her death, expressing her support of Nelson Mandela and equality for blacks. It was a sobering moment when her killers realized that Amy had been on their side.

My husband and I also saw this story on TV's "60 Minutes." It was reported that instead of being angry and hateful and demanding revenge, Amy's parents decided to do what they could to better the lives of the people where their daughter had served and given her life. With their own funds, Amy's parents initiated programs for South African youth and adults in various trades which would create self-sufficiency.

For example, Amy's parents established a bakery with state-of-the-art equipment. They brought in all the raw materials necessary for doing business and provided classes to teach the employees how to make bakery goods and manage the business. Amy's parents also introduced several other programs that helped foster a sense of purpose and hope for those living in the ghettos. Their time and selfless effort inspired amazement.

My husband and I were very touched by Amy's parents' ability to turn their daughter's tragedy into a monumental triumph. Their contribution to the well-being of those they helped was soul-stirring. But, more importantly, the growth Amy's parents experienced personally, through forgiving and opening their hearts, was awe-inspiring and truly uplifting.

We each have this basic goodness within us. If we possess a strong enough desire to shift our focus, we can re-discover it. After all, we each brought that goodness with us. When we understand this, our nature instinctively yields to a higher and greater cause—a higher purpose (as with Amy's parents). Our capacity for loving and supporting others increases dramatically. We can look, and if our eyes are truly open, we will see and appreciate the magnificent importance of each individual—including our own *Self*. When our actions stem from love and understanding (from our heart), we are less condemning, more forgiving, more accepting, and more compassionate.

There may be those of us, however, who have been so abused that we are still staggering from emotional trauma or pain that has not yet healed. Could our feelings of resentment, anger, hatred or bitterness have such deep tentacles that it's difficult to see or feel beyond our misery? Perhaps these feelings serve us and are such a major part of our identity and existence that we would feel lost without them. If any of the foregoing conditions exist within us, healing will need to be accomplished before we can re-discover and re-connect with our basic goodness.

Someone may say, But you don't know how much I have suffered because of such and such or so and so. Or, You have no idea what I have been through. How can you expect me to overcome this?

It is true that many people have experienced horrible trauma. And it may be they have not yet had the opportunity of finding help, or have not known that they needed assistance in healing these experiences. Some people have suffered physically or sexually; some have suffered mentally or emotionally; others have suffered spiritually—or all of the above.

There are countless kinds of suffering. Each person's experience will be distinctive, for there are as many stories as there are people. Despite the differences, despite the extremes, each of us eventually needs to deal with the rage and pain (even though it may be justified) if we wish to regain peace and harmony within. Only by going inside ourselves can these feelings be healed—healing and forgiving come from within.

If you have experienced abuse and your suffering and rage are extreme, the process may take longer. It may progress in stages; but if you choose, healing *can* take place. Know that you are not alone. Others are on the path with you, working to overcome some of the same obstacles. Many who have experienced the ultimate suffering have been able to turn their suffering into extraordinary growth.

Never give up! You have what it takes or you wouldn't still be alive and reading this book. Call back your *Will* and allow your Spirit, your Higher Self, to take charge of your life. With the help of God, all things are possible.

> If you think you are beaten, you are.
> If you think you dare not, you don't.
> If you like to win but think you can't,
> It's almost certain that you won't.
> Life's battles don't always go
> To the stronger woman or man,
> But sooner or later, those who win
> Are those who think they can.
>
> —Unknown

The following is a news story my husband and I viewed one evening. This story is a classic example of someone turning horrible physical suffering into extraordinary growth and a personal victory.

Kim Chun was only a small girl during the war in Viet Nam. During a bombing raid on one of the cities, a building which housed many children was hit. Pictures of this incident were shown with screaming children running down the road naked, their burning skin hanging from their bodies.

Kim was one of the more critically injured children, with horrible third degree burns covering most of her body. She wasn't expected to live. But she did—undergoing innumerable skin graft operations throughout her life. Terribly disfigured over much of her body, she hardly knew a day without excruciating pain. Still, she maintained a beautiful, positive attitude about life.

As an adult, married and with two children, Kim eventually came to live in the United States. Her constant dream had been to find the pilot of the plane who dropped the bomb that caused her disfigurement, to let him know that she forgave him. This dream was a driving force in Kim.

After learning about Kim, we heard the pilot's story. When he saw the pictures of those children running down the road screaming as their flesh continued to burn, he was almost inconsolable, recognizing that he had been the one who created this scene and caused their excruciating pain and subsequent scars. His remorse and feelings of guilt for this act never left him. He eventually became a minister, hoping he could somehow atone for the pain and scars of that horrible day.

Kim and the pilot finally connected many years after the tragedy. I remember the tears streaming down our faces, as we saw the healing balm and closure created for both of them through Kim's ability to forgive. Her profoundly beautiful example illustrates the magnificent power we all have within to free constricted or inharmonious energy—to forgive.

CHAPTER 8

Would You Like Another Avenue?

Never apologize for showing feeling.
When you do, you apologize for the truth.

—Benjamin Disraeli

If you would like additional methods for processing your feelings, this chapter will offer other simple and effective do-it-yourself possibilities. These processes may not go to the same depth as Scripting; nonetheless, they are beneficial and have proven extremely effective in resolving negative energy.

Let's say that you have unresolved feelings smoldering inside. Whether or not you consciously remember their origin, sequester yourself from the rest of the world. *Be* with these energies and the feelings they generate. *Be* with these feelings throughout your entire body! You don't like what they are doing to you while submerged, so encourage these feelings to come to the surface. Concentrate on them. Breathe deeply. *Feeeeel* the feelings with every breath and in every molecule of your Be-ing! Just keep feeling them.

When they reach their peak let these feelings out, however they want to be expressed.

Though you may not like exposing your true feelings (possibly you *think* you shouldn't *feel* this way), if you feel like screaming, "I hate you, I hate you, I hate you," do it with all the strength you can muster! Direct that energy toward the person responsible for causing your feelings of hate. Even though you may no longer feel hatred toward the responsible person, keep in mind that the aspect of you reeling with the pain of hate and needing to cry out could be your Child. Let the hurting Child finally have an avenue of release! You are doing this for your own healing and survival. Give yourself permission to release the hate or whatever has been pent up for who knows how long.

Feelings that have been buried for any length of time usually carry numerous appendages which seldom exist on a conscious level. If your tender psyche was mistreated when you were helpless to oppose the violation, countless feelings may have spun off from the initial one. For instance, possible appendages from being violated may find voice as "How dare you take advantage of me in my innocence, in my inability to protect myself! Take that, and that, and that." (Here's where hitting a pillow works well.)

Another example: "I didn't do what you accused me of doing! Still, you mercilessly humiliated and brought me down in front of others!" (Cry, cry, cry.) This process is referred to as *Vocalizing*. Give those buried feelings permission to voice their pain!

When the need to fight back, to be heard or understood was not granted expression, there remained a part of you (the Child? the Female? The Male?) desperately aching to do that very thing—express itself! Often the expression you need now requires a response you were unable to perform during the initial violation. If pounding on a big pillow or hitting a punching bag helps the process of discharging pent up, constricted feelings, do it! (Be gentle with the walls, though.)

What you're feeling might not be hate, but whatever the feeling is, "own" the e-motion. Remember, these feelings are not a reflection of your Divine *Self*. In actuality, this *Self* has been desirous of resolving these feelings for a long time. That's why they are triggered and keep manifesting through your thoughts, words, attitudes, beliefs, and actions. Your feelings are doing their best to get your attention. They want you to know your inner enemy. Allow them. Embrace them. And remember that you are still a good person.

At the same time, realize the damage these negative feelings have created inside of you. Feel the feelings for the final time and embrace any cleansing pain which may surface. It's only temporary and it helps with the healing.

Remember, these feelings have been registering and compounding in unhealed areas or aspects of your Be-ing. They are the parts of you that froze in time when there was no way of expressing or resolving the trauma.

Some people seem to have a pretty good "handle" on life. They take things in stride and usually recognize their strengths and weaknesses. They know how to approach and resolve challenges. They know how to maintain a positive attitude. Periodically, though, they may also have need to deal with feelings from a challenging situation. When this occurs, the feelings usually resonate with something from the past which requires introspection.

Realize that often our challenges and the resultant feelings are a wake-up call to re-assess how we are doing. E-motion still smoldering inside reminds us that we have unsuccessfully processed feelings not only at the time of the original incident, but now as an adult. Concentrate on the feeling at hand to resolve the current challenge. Along with Scripting, you might enjoy Vocalizing as a means to change this energy and release your frustration.

During an experiential process in one of my workshops, the attendees, one at a time, participated in an activity relating to their earlier years. With no prompting whatsoever, and with her eyes closed, Merradyth, 48, started clenching her fists and jaw. Under her breath, she began, "I hate you, I hate you, I hate you!"

Merradyth was definitely not a hateful person, so at the onset, I didn't know who she was addressing. But it soon became apparent. Her voice grew louder and louder as she pounded her legs with each declaration. She had a lot to unleash, so I encouraged her to continue as forcefully as she needed. Her daughter provided a big sofa pillow to soften the blows to her legs.

A victim of incest and the eldest of 18 children, Merradyth had learned at an early age that it didn't pay to feel. She had quite ably disarmed herself by pretending nothing was wrong. (Trauma victims almost always embrace the false notion that if they are quiet, the problem might go away). In a super-human effort, Merradyth took upon herself the family secrets. She unconsciously expended much of her energy being the "peacemaker"—the caretaker who kept things running smoothly. While assuming this role, Merradyth effectively turned off her feelings and ultimately lost touch with them. Throughout most of her life, Merradyth never cried, never became truly angry, never felt real joy, sorrow, or anything. Yet people were attracted to her. She was always pleasant, never became ruffled, and always seemed in total control.

The experience of screaming hatred at her father lasted over 20 minutes. Merradyth was finally able to let out the unconscious, buried, hidden, and hate-charged energy the *Child* and *Female* aspects had unknowingly felt toward her father for so many years.

Merradyth realized her pent up hatred was finally abating when the words "I hate you" became less and less audible. The charge of energy was losing its place in her heart. Merradyth's release was very, very healing—not only for her, but for her two young adult daughters. They witnessed the release of the electrical charge their mother had masked and repressed for more than 40 years. The daughters cried and felt the pain right along with their mother. They were also victims of their grandfather's abuse.

Remember, if you have had a strong urge to hit the person who caused you pain, use something (a big pillow perhaps) to help release the anger brought on by your helplessness—by your inability to change the situation or stop that person. Release all the pent up energy you can by hitting the pillow with the goal of finally discharging the old feelings. As you perform this action, think about your incapacity to defend, protect, or speak for yourself at the time of the incident. Hitting was either not allowed or you were physically incapable of defending yourself. Aspects of you have been waiting a long time to be expressed and heard. Allow the expression!

If you feel a need to unleash feelings, isolate yourself and do it! Scream (or whatever) until the energy of that feeling is totally diffused—until you no longer have the desire to scream. Do it for yourself, now! It's all right. If you prefer releasing pent up energy another way, do it.

Your core Be-ing does not enjoy harboring unresolved negative feelings, for these feelings have taken you from the truth of who you really are! This is why there is such an inner conflict. And because these feelings are negatively charged vibrational energies, they can be painful. They may have been bottled up for years. Expressing these old feelings doesn't make you a bad person, but helps in your emotional healing.

When you have unlocked and unleashed pent up feelings, look into your eyes in the mirror. Script the negative feelings you just released, cleansing any lingering residue. Fill the void created by the unleashing with a positive feeling of your choice. Forgiveness, love, mercy, and compassion are very appropriate. The main objective of this process is to transform negative energies into positive, thus bringing you back to the intrinsic purity of your heart. Lighten your load by giving this process your full and loving attention.

In *Walking Between the Worlds,* Gregg Braden shares something revealing and profound.

Shifting your body chemistry by shifting your viewpoint [by shifting your feelings and thoughts], is perhaps the single most powerful tool that you have available to you for the remainder of this lifetime.

Researchers have recently demonstrated to the western

world a phenomenon that has been taught . . . for thousands of years. New data now supports the idea that human emotion [feelings and thoughts] determines the actual patterning of DNA within the body. Furthermore, laboratory demonstrations have shown that DNA determines how patterns of light, expressed as matter, surround the human body. Imagine the implications.

Stated another way, researchers have discovered that the arrangement of matter (atoms, bacteria, viruses, climate, even other people) surrounding your body, is directly linked to the feeling and emotion from within your body!

. . . Beyond microcircuit technology, beyond genetic splicing and drug induced engineering, without exception this relationship between your physical body (DNA) and emotion represents the single most sophisticated technology to ever grace this world through the expression of our bodies.

Our own science now has demonstrated that DNA, your DNA, is directly tied to your ability to forgive, allow and love through the expression of your life. The science of loving, forgiving and allowing is nothing new. The technology underlying love and forgiveness is an ancient as well as universal science, known today as compassion. *Your ability to express forgiveness, allowing others the outcome of their own experience, without changing the nature of who you are, is a hallmark of the highest levels of life mastery.*" (Emphasis added)

CHAPTER 9

Liberating Your "Self"

The journey of a thousand miles begins
and ends with one step.

—Lao Tsu

Given the hurt and pain to which some of us have been subjected, we may find ourselves unknowingly—but naturally—engaging in self-pity, feeling that no one has ever had it as bad or as hard as we have. Remember, there is always someone out there who has experienced worse and lived to tell about it. This does not diminish the fact that some people experience unimaginable pain and suffering, but it may help to know we are not alone.

I have often wondered how some of my clients lived through their suffering and torment.

If we engage in self-pity, we need to consider that it may be the doorway into a destructive attitude of living. Recognize too, that we can accept or reject the feeling of self-pity—no one forces us there. By realizing that self-pity keeps us from moving forward, then making the decision to resist its downward spiral, we can become victors over the defeatist attitude it represents. I'm reminded of Christopher Reeve's beautiful attitude and his courageous fight against the paralysis that has been his misfortune.

Ignorance of what we are doing is what gives self-pity such power. If we choose to focus on the injustice, the hurt, the bad luck, or the lack in our lives, we continue drawing these conditions to us. We re-create the same challenges time and time again. Yes, without exception, what we put out into the ethers returns to us; therefore, what we experience is never simply luck. We innocently design our experiences—the desirable and the undesirable—through our feelings, thoughts, and attitudes.

Within every difficult situation, every seeming failure, every discouraging loss or heart-rending setback is locked the great, miraculous power of complete, triumphant, progressive, magnificent achievement. How many of us know someone injured in a terrible accident or involved in a tragic mishap who lived through the pain of healing their body and emotions to become a better person?

Instead of focusing on misfortunes or the seeming unfairness in life, look around and take tally of all the things for which you are grateful. Focus on the positive and express your heartfelt gratitude continually. You will accelerate your potential for healing and more readily recognize your inharmonious choices. As you express gratitude you will also discover it to be the eternal law of positive increase.

When confronted with a challenge, ask yourself, How did I contribute to the evolution of this dilemma? Remember, everything happening to you is happening for a reason. If you ask what the reason is often enough, you will discover the answer. You will find the lesson you are to learn—the gift (pre-sent) you have presented to yourself. Look deep within and find what needs to be re-formed or re-stored. Then choose a more positive feeling or a different frame of reference. If the desired change isn't forthcoming through understanding it intellectually, Script for it. Doing so is very empowering.

If you do not identify with self-pity, you may identify with the need to always be "right" about everything—or knowing everything there is to know! A person with this mindset usually dominates the conversation no matter where he/she is or with whom he/she is talking. Have you ever known this type of individual? Very often they won't listen to anything someone else has to offer. They can hardly wait for you to finish talking so they can add their two cents worth. Often they are totally insensitive to how others are responding to them. They seldom allow anyone input and seem interested only in what they have to say.

Bless their hearts. If they only realized how much they're missing in life by not being open to the possibility that someone else might have something to offer. Think how much they miss by not being open to others. Why is there such a strong need in them to "know it," to be "right," to have the last word all the time?

Could it be that somewhere, sometime they were extremely humiliated or totally stripped of their dignity? Were they chastened or told they were wrong? Is it possible they subconsciously seek a resolution to that humiliation? Is that why they act out and seem insensitive? Is their *Child* striving to never be wrong so as not to be humiliated again?

If you see this person in yourself, look at the frustration, anxiety, agitation, and uncertainty this mindset creates.

Scripting for "the feelings that cause me the need to be right" can truly assist you in changing this characteristic. For example

> "Please locate the origin of the feelings that cause me the *need* to be right all the time." Replace with, "I give myself permission to be wrong. I allow others to be in charge of conversations. It's all right for me to be quiet and not say a word. I enjoy hearing what other people have to say. I learn from them. I don't need to let every one know how much I know. I choose feeling peaceful. I feel peaceful. I am peaceful."

It is worth noting that we learn more by listening than we do by talking. The old adage, Still water runs deep, is indeed true.

If this Scripting doesn't exactly describe the way you feel, supply your own words. Keep applying the Script until you notice an energy shift—until you can allow other people center stage, until you no longer feel the need to prove something or be right about everything. Script until you feel peaceful.

Another mindset prevalent in today's society is the need to be in control. This characteristic is found in people who either "go ballistic" or pout when something happens differently than they have planned—something that isn't on their agenda. There seems to be a belief in these people that they must be in control of everyone around them, spouse, children, co-workers, anyone with whom they associate.

When we lose contact with the Love that we are, the need to control takes over. Do you know someone with these characteristics? What seems to be their motivation?

I have found that the controlling person may have had their *Will* taken from them early in life. Perhaps a traumatic incident occurred which they could do nothing about; where they felt powerless and were unable to handle the trauma.

Maybe they found themselves in an extremely threatening situation, or a series of them. Perhaps their parents argued or divorced or a loved one died. If any of these experiences occurred, something inside vowed, By darn, I'm never going to allow myself to be this helpless ever again!

Such individuals couldn't prevent the undesirable experiences as a youth. Naturally a strong desire now drives the adult to be in charge and see that things happen according to their desires or agenda. In other words, their mind set may be, I'm never going to let myself hurt that much. Or perhaps, The people I love are never going to hurt! I'm going to make sure things go the way I want.

Some individuals believe there are only two ways of doing things—the wrong way and my way. They want you to conform to their world. This allows them to feel comfortable so they won't experience confrontation or challenge. These people can be inflexible about everything! At the same time, they have suggestions for fixing everyone around them.

The my-way-or-the-wrong-way attitude alienates most of the human race. Consequently, this type of person may assume the attitude of martyr, victim, persecutor or rescuer. If, for example, these individuals happen to live with someone who doesn't conform to their way, the persona of victim emerges, convinced it has to suffer as the martyr. This pattern continues unless there is effective intervention.

People with these varied characteristics obviously don't like change, and they are constantly challenged when they live around people who enjoy change. Often their loved ones feel like they are going crazy due to the ups and downs of the varied personas. Consider . . . what could the feelings be that caused the burdensome imbalance which created the martyr, victim, persecutor and rescuer?

Perhaps free expression was discredited or never allowed as a youth. Possibly the child's efforts were not valued by parents. Maybe they were forced to march to someone else's drum beat. We can never be sure of the underlying reasons. That's why it's so important to strive for understanding before we expect to be understood. We have no idea what people have had to experience, nor what mind-set has been created and perpetuated through false perceptions, conditioning, family patterns and idiosyncrasies.

The cumulative effects of varied dysfunctions can cause people to either examine their lives or go deeper into denial. Perhaps you know this type. They insist on living in their own safe world, never facing the fact that their childhood, school years, marriage, or relationship with their children could possibly use healing. According to them, everything is perfectly fine just the way it is. Does this resonate with you?

If so, has your whole life been vested in projecting "the perfect family" image? Where has this attitude taken you? Has it made you truly happy? Has it been productive? Or are you still putting out fires that might dispel the *myth* of the perfect family? Consider the effort expended while putting out those fires.

Is there something wrong with the way things actually

are—with the truth? Recall, if you will, the scripture that says, "Know the truth, and the truth shall make you free" (John 8:32). Perhaps the truth is too frightening or too embarrassing. Would removing yourself from the mode you have established cause you an identity crisis? If so, ask yourself, What kind of a prison have I built around me?

Have you ever heard the saying, It's none of my business what other people think of me? When I first heard these words, contemplated their meaning, then internalized them, it was one of the greatest days of my life! Talk about being freed from prison. This was the beginning of my liberation!

By honoring and liberating the *Self,* by moving out of complacency and facing the actuality that there *is* something in our life that does need changing—that does need correcting—we begin truthfully enjoying our life!

Change is a very scary word. Many of us feel extremely threatened by change. Thomas Carlyle, however, shares some wonderful words of wisdom that help us see it from another perspective: "The greatest of faults—is to be conscious of none."

Bill, a former 34-year-old client, was adopted as a baby. For many years he experienced his share of trials. Deep feelings of emptiness could never be filled. When he was in his mid thirties Bill's parents decided to look for his biological mother, hoping to fill the void in Bill's life.

When they located his family of origin, Bill was very excited to talk on the phone with the brother and sister he had never known. Then he spoke with the mother who gave him birth.

About a month after locating his family, Bill was able to meet them. Everything seemed to be just as he had hoped.

His long lost relatives assured him that they were a stable, successful, and functional family. He took them at their word. But just before Bill returned home, he learned there were a few skeletons in the closet that the family had failed to mention earlier. When this happened, Bill became extremely hurt and angry! All he had longed for was the truth from them. He felt he could handle it, regardless of what it might be.

The bomb dropped in Bill's lap just before his visit ended—that his family hadn't been completely truthful with him—was almost more than he could bear. He felt totally betrayed by those he had hoped he could trust and depend upon for strength! The reality was shattering, and at this point, Bill very much regretted his pursuit to discover his roots.

Evidently, Bill's biological family was unable to "own" the truth. Who knows why. Perhaps they were afraid that Bill would not accept them if he knew about the family skeletons. Whatever the reason, it is unfortunate that this long-lost family didn't realize the cleansing and freeing power of truth.

If healing your life is your desire, you need to understand that taking responsibility and being accountable for your own stuff is possibly more liberating than anything you have ever experienced. If you haven't been *speaking your truth*, you haven't been enjoying life as it is meant to be enjoyed. And because you may have allowed your *Self* to fall into the false security of old behavior patterns, stepping out of your comfort zone into the unknown may be scary. Staying in that comfort zone, however, truly limits any possible growth you might achieve.

Lift the lid from that box in which you have encased yourself. Or peek over that wall you have been erecting. Look around and determine the best direction to take for un-covering the part of life you have been missing! Ask yourself, How would it be to live life to the fullest?

Be ready to own your faults, your mistakes, your errors. Be ready to face, as well as to admit, the truth. It's okay! Does it make you less of a person? Most assuredly not! It adds to your stature. Reflect on how you feel when some-one admits to you that they are, or have been wrong, or when someone apologizes to you. Do you think less or more of them?

If you would really like to see deep, deep healing occur, instead of just saying, "I'm sorry" to someone when the occasion calls for it, ask, "Will you forgive me?" It will astound you what can be accomplished by asking, "Will you forgive me?"

When you say "I'm sorry" to someone, they do not need to internalize or acknowledge whether they accept that apology or not. You, in essence, are taking full responsibility onto yourself, for the situation. Whereas, when you ask, "Will you forgive me?" the other person shares in the responsibility of clearing any negative energy between the two of you. The healing then goes in both directions. Even if they don't answer you out loud, in their heart and mind will come a *yes* or a *no*. And it doesn't matter what they reply nor whether their reply is silent or audible. You have done your part by bringing your *Self* to ask for their forgiveness. At the same time, if you have truly let go of your pride and removed your *Self* from your ego, you have also allowed the Truth of your Be-ing to come through. What an accomplishment! What a wonderful feeling! And believe me, it is.

Every person on the face of the earth has their own set of faults! Don't condemn yourself for gathering negative energy on your journey. It's part of life's plan. Experiencing the negative, darker energies is necessary so you can come to understand and appreciate the nature of the positive, lighter energies. It's what you choose doing with the negative energies (faults, mistakes, and errors) that counts.

So ask yourself the question, Am I Be-ing complacent and letting the negative co-exist with me from day to day? Am I remembering that energy/matter can be changed? Am I determined to accomplish this mighty change?

Re-solving our less than glorious feelings, thoughts, attitudes and beliefs gives us a whole new perspective on life. And Be-ing accountable can be an exciting new adventure—almost like a game! Life relinquishes its heaviness. We let go of needing to control or needing to be right about everything. We realize that if things are not pleasant at the present moment, there's always the option for change—even if it's just our perception that requires the change. When we desire peace, changing our feelings—thereby changing our mind—is a very small price to pay for achieving that peace.

Allow yourself to experience the astounding difference these changes make in your life! As you are moving through this re-formation, your family and friends will not even recognize you as the same human Be-ing.

CHAPTER 10

Who's to Blame?

A man may fail many times,
but he isn't a failure until he begins to blame somebody else.

—Unknown

Have you ever known someone who seemed to stand still on their journey through life, regardless of a strong desire to change for the better? Could this person be stuck—and in their "stuckness" believe someone or something is keeping them from achieving the changes they would like? Perhaps this individual blames circumstances or another person for the inability to move forward.

Some of us may believe that the things giving us problems in life are out there—on the outside of us—like an outside enemy. Outside enemy? Is that how we refer to someone or something upon which we place blame? What we don't understand is that *we* created this enemy, only this enemy is not on the outside. It's on the inside. Could this be why blaming someone else seldom solves a problem? Are we pointing our finger at the wrong enemy? Is this also the reason that blaming keeps us from acquiring the wisdom we came here to gain?

In essence blaming, or pointing our finger, is saying that we totally absolve our *Self* of any responsibility in the matter. At the same time, we automatically and unwittingly assign ourselves to the miserable role of victim. By feeling we are a victim, our unconscious attitude becomes *We are not responsible for our own plight.* Thus, we imagine someone or something else as being responsible. Someone or something out there must be our enemy! This view renders us powerless because we allow that someone to be in command—to be in control. By giving up stewardship of our responsibilities to someone else, we relinquish our God-given power—and our Will, as well.

A perfect example is reflected in the circumstances surrounding the death of Princess Diana. Initially, no one knew the details of the tragedy. Most of us would like to have known the cause immediately. We would like to have had every detail spelled out so there would be no need to speculate—so we could have put the blame where it belonged. We would have felt justified in pointing a finger and saying, "Shame, shame on you."

In the final analysis though, most of us knew in our hearts that had this woman been spared the unrelenting pursuit of photographers hoping to sell her pictures to the tabloids, she could have enjoyed, like most of us, a normal evening out. And . . . this woman might still be alive today.

While watching countless reports about Princess Diana, I observed this unfortunate side of our human nature—the need to place blame on someone. How many of us would like to have blamed the driver of the car or blamed the paparazzi? If we could blame someone, then it would take us off the hook as to our own accountability. If we could blame someone else for this tragedy, then it would be all right for us to have read, and continue to read, the tabloids. If they—the driver or the paparazzi—could be blamed, then our conscience would be cleared. How sad. But the most grievous part of the whole scenario is that it was all done in the name of what? In other words, was her pursuit that night justified?

Unfortunately, most of us are not aware (unless we stop to think about it) that we often have a *need* to blame. If the conditions in our lives are not to our liking, then we want to blame someone or something out there. Yes, let's blame our outer enemy. In reality our inner enemy, whom we don't see, is generating this need to blame. But, if we don't know there is an inner enemy, we certainly don't realize when we are hiding behind that enemy instead of taking responsibility for our own creation. We haven't understood who our real enemy is!

There are those who have been conditioned to obediently and automatically take the blame, regardless of the circumstances. When a person recognizes this, usually in their adulthood, they can change the behavior and the belief that drives it. The ability to do so is an important principle to understand, as the belief is perpetuated by the inner enemy.

If we haven't been aware of this enemy, then naturally we haven't known where it resides. Unfortunately, without our being aware, this inner enemy has been allowed to slowly re-place the Love that we are. How? By not knowing that our negative, buried feelings need re-solving. Because we have innocently allowed these unresolved feelings to occupy our minds and hearts, their energies have amassed and created their own heavy personality. They have obscured our True Self—the Love that we are.

If we aren't being governed by our True Self, then by whom are we being governed? We are being governed by the personality that has obscured our True Self and become our inner enemy. This enemy usually feels threatened by the least little thing. It works against us instead of with us. Because the human psyche automatically views this enemy as being outside of us, we unknowingly project our negative (enemy) feelings outward. We project them onto other people and place blame on anything and everything we possibly can.

Somewhere along life's journey, most of us were conditioned or felt the need to exhibit a brave front—to play the game of life. We followed what we thought were the rules, even if they were unspoken. We learned to keep quiet instead of speaking our truth—instead of rocking the boat, taking a stand. Consequently, we've tip-toed around each other's sensitivities, fearful of saying anything that would hurt someone's feelings or cause discomfort. Yes, we've slowly put on a mask so that in our innocent self-doubt and need to say the proper thing (often something we don't truly feel), we can be acceptable in everyone's eyes. We didn't understand that it wasn't our sole responsibility to make those around us happy or comfortable.

The unawareness of the mask we are wearing—the mask we ourselves are hiding behind—is an attribute of our inner enemy. This mask only covers over our problems, deluding us to believe that everything is just fine.

Our children don't wear a mask, but it doesn't take long before conditioning helps them create one.

By remaining unaware and ignoring the inner enemy residing in us, our internal darkness eventually becomes destructive. How does this happen?

Since we view our enemy as being "out there," that enemy will always appear in the guise of another. In other words, *any hostility that originates in us takes the form of hostility towards others.* We blame other people for things that go wrong and for things we don't like. For some reason it doesn't occur to us to look inside our *Self!*

What some of us haven't understood is that placing blame never solved a problem. Blaming only heightens the problem. When you think about it, isn't placing the blame on others taking the easy way out? Yes, blaming keeps us from taking responsibility and accountability. By not Be-ing responsible and accountable, our True Self slowly loses its identity and erodes away. When we don't accept and face the strong possibility that there is an inner enemy, this very enemy runs the show—and as long as it is running the show, we are stuck!

We may try to run away from our inner enemy, but it goes with us where ever we go. Hence, we keep feeling the same negative feelings, experiencing the same frustrations and the same challenges. We continue repeating the same unproductive patterns and have difficulty resolving our problems and moving forward.

By giving our *Self* permission to acknowledge this inner enemy, half the battle is won. However, until we embrace that part of us as our teacher—as our best friend—we are unable to learn what is imperative about our *Self.* We are unable to un-cover the truth of our Be-ing and experience life to the fullest.

Once again, if we desire Be-ing a more loving and peaceful person, the prerequisite is to Be responsible and accountable for our own feelings, thoughts, words, attitudes, and behavior. If we objectively pay attention, we will be able to see within our *Self* and discern our inner enemy. Then we can discover our mask and lovingly remove it. When the mask is gone, we are no longer the actor. We become the author of our life.

We sharpen our emotional saw (awareness) by recognizing and acknowledging when we miss the mark; by owning our less than glorious traits—our imperfections and weaknesses. Always remember, it's all right that we have imperfections. However, only by facing them and resolving the feelings that brought us there can our inner conflicts and contradictions relinquish their hold. Owning and resolving our negative feelings also raises our vibrational frequencies. This allows a major shift in all areas of our life and propels us forward on our transformational journey.

Let us bring this concept into the first person. Please read the following slowly.

> That which I have ignored or been blind to, which is vital and important in understanding my own personality, I unconsciously see in others. And usually it's something for which I feel disdain or fear. This projection of something in myself onto others is done quite unconsciously on my part, which is why I always seem so innocent in my own eyes. The projection of my enemy onto another individual distorts my relationship with him and forces that person to carry my psychological burden, which is most unfair to him.
>
> —John Sanford, *The Kingdom Within*

Sometimes we participate in this projection with our own children. John Sanford goes on to tell of one rigid, moralistic woman who projected onto her daughter all of her own unrecognized sensuality. From puberty on, she viewed the girl as cheap and worthless, a problem in the making. So it was no surprise when, at the age of sixteen, the daughter became pregnant out of wedlock. For the mother, it was a validation of what she had known all along—a self-fulfilling prophecy. For the daughter, it was a fate forced upon her by the projection of her mother's own shadowy nature, which the girl had been compelled to carry and live out. It also validated the maxims: *The projection upon which we dwell long enough, we create;* and, *that which we fear we draw to us.* Since the woman could only see her daughter as a problem in the making, naturally she helped propel her daughter into that role.

How sad. But you see, the mother didn't know any better. She wasn't armed with an understanding of what caused her feelings, her beliefs and, therefore, her behavior. How unfortunate that she wasn't aware of her Real enemy—the enemy within. Once again, according to Thomas Carlyle, *"The greatest of faults, is to be conscious of none."*

John Sanford also shares what happens when the projection of our inner enemy onto another takes place on a collective, racial or international basis. This projection is particularly destructive as history repeatedly shows. For instance, having identified themselves as a super-race and a divinely superior people, the Nazis no longer recognized their own hidden, inferior qualities. Therefore, they projected these qualities onto the Jews. The Jews were forced to carry for the Nazis what the Nazis would not see in themselves. Consequently, the Jews carried the burden of hate, fear, and loathing that the Nazis, in fact, had for themselves. The ensuing wholesale and horrible slaughter of the Jews was a futile attempt by the Nazis to exterminate their projected inner enemy.

So, you might ask, what is the solution? The basic steps for dealing with the inner enemy are

1) Accept the possibility of the inner enemy's existence;
2) Realize that you, along with everyone else, may unknowingly be harboring an inner enemy;
3) Acknowledge and Own the inner enemy within your Be-ing. (Having this enemy doesn't make you a bad person);
4) Understand and Be Grateful for the teacher your inner enemy has been, and continues to be;
5) Be vigilant in recognizing and dealing with your inner enemy every time it raises its ugly head.

Look for this enemy in your daily words, thoughts, feelings, attitudes, beliefs, actions, and behavior as these are the places it makes itself known. When you are truly intent on discovering and uprooting your inner enemy, you will pay particular attention each day.

In other words, if we desire to eliminate our dislike or hatred of supposed enemies, we must start by looking at the reflection of our *Self* in that enemy. We only dislike in others what we dislike in our *Self*. If the quality we hate were not in our *Self*, we could not see it in another person, Likewise, if the quality we love were not in our *Self*, we could not see it in someone else.

Until we understand and accept this truth, we continue

carrying the burden of our counterfeit personalities—our inner enemy.

Paraphrasing John Sanford again: We literally carry this enemy in our own hearts. We hate him because he contradicts the truth of who we are. We fear if we acknowledge him as our own, he will take us over completely. The precise opposite is true. By *not* acknowledging our inner enemy, we fall into his power as he mocks us in our futile efforts to be rid of the imaginary outside enemy. We would rather get rid of those presumed enemies who carry the projection of our own darkness, so we will no longer be reminded of it—so we will no longer be faced with our own dragons, nor be responsible for them. Somehow, if we believe the outer enemy is gone, we won't need to be accountable for our own biases, weaknesses, and incorrect perceptions. How sadly disabled we've been, not knowing about our inner enemy.

Unfortunately, by continually blaming others for our discomfort and believing they are the enemy, our own negative energies keep compounding because they aren't being resolved. While blaming, we perpetuate and amplify the characteristics of that very enemy we are striving to eliminate. Consequently, what started out as an innocent scratch becomes a huge dent! Perhaps we even allow it our whole focus and eventually become completely blinded by it.

There is something else the inner enemy accomplishes. It keeps us in a state of separateness from others. This is plain to see when we observe some of the hate groups in society today.

Perhaps we now understand why acknowledging the enemy as our own is the beginning of being released from his power and finding his constructive side.

In her book *Courage to Live Your Truth,* cover artist, Valerieann J. Skinner, shares her unique approach to better understanding the inner enemy. She puts things in perspective from another direction. You may be interested in her view.

All of our lives we encounter a constant stream of what we term "good" and "bad," "right" and "wrong." At an early age we begin deciding which things we like to experience and which things we don't. We tend to avoid the unpleasant whenever possible and seek to experience that which is agreeable to us. Even though we get quite efficient at avoiding most of the undesirable things in life, it never fails that things "just happen"—things that are painful, heartbreaking, and difficult to deal with. Because these things are usually perceived as totally unfair and undeserved, we tend to ask the question, "Why me?" But it may be helpful to pose a different question, "Why are we here having *any* experiences, good *or* bad?" To answer this, let's go back to childhood.

When a child is first born, does she know what "warm" is? She experiences warmth as she is snuggled in a blanket in her mother's arms, but as a concept, as temperature, it has no meaning for her. Eventually, as she begins to toddle, she is told not to touch something because "it is hot." But what does *that* mean? She figures it's "bad," if the tone of her mother's voice is anything to go by; but until she actually experiences hot, that's all she knows.

Can you recall your first experience of hot, or did you totally avoid it because your mother told you to? It's not likely. Being blessed with a healthy dose of curiosity, the child in us eventually "experiences" hot by touching something hot with our fingers. So now that the child has experienced hot, does this school us in knowing what "warm" is? I don't think so.

For the purpose of this story, let us now say that she has always lived in an environment of 72°—in warmth. This, and having burned her finger, is all she knows of temperature. But because she has been warm all of her life, she takes that aspect of it for granted. It still has no real meaning for her—not the way "hot" does.

Winter arrives and the child is now old enough to go out to play in the snow. Her mother bundles her up, and out she goes. After a period of time her fingers and toes begin tingling and they feel quite uncomfortable—she has discovered cold! She comes in to get warm, because she realizes that she would prefer a temperature closer to the hot side of things. And now she knows hot and cold and even that there is something in between—warm. She is also learning about "good" and "bad," and that sometimes the same thing can be either. As she sits in front of the fire, what at first seemed bad about hot is now starting to feel pretty good. And as she gets older, she learns that just as warm fits somewhere between hot and cold, there is a wide range of things between the extremes of good and bad. She would have learned none of these things if she had spent her entire life in the house in a constant state of warmth, protected from all experience.

We don't all have to burn our fingers in order to know what hot is. Many are able to avoid experiencing extreme opposites simply by observing the experiences of others. It was not I who touched a hot stove as a child, it was my brother. I have avoided many undesirable things by heeding the warnings of my parents. However, experiencing opposing forces is unavoidable in this physical world. There is polarity in all things.

Having now explored something that is familiar to us all, allow me to take it a step further. Love is the true nature of our being. If we were *Love* before we came to earth, and that was all we had ever experienced, would we—anymore than the child did of warmth—know what Love or our true Self really was? Wouldn't we be taking it for granted? Would we have had a full knowledge of Love without something to compare it to? Could this possibly have something to do with why we are here experiencing all that we are experiencing? Could it be that this is the very purpose of our existence—coming to know our Self, our true nature, gaining the knowledge and the wisdom that we could not gain in our pre-mortal existence?

What if we divided the light from the dark, the good from the bad, the love from the fear? What if we divided our totality, the whole essence of our being (Love), into all of its various parts and pieces—into opposites? Would the experience of hate, pain, and misery give us something with which to measure love, pleasure, and joy? Would we then be able to *consciously* and fully experience that love and that joy—who we really are?

Assuming we were whole in the beginning (meaning the Love that we are), could we now be experiencing the separation that has unknowingly been created in the various parts of our *Self*? This would mean that even what we perceive as *evil* and *negative* is as much a part of us as the *love* and *goodness*. If indeed this is so, what good would it do to remain in fear of our negative elements? Aren't we then running away from our *Self*?

What if the very things we are most afraid of—the evils we perceive "out there"—are truly a most important ingredient in returning us to our wholeness, to Love? Could it be that the reason the things we fear seem to chase us so intensely, is because they are that Love, helping us see the other parts and pieces of ourselves so that we will then *know* what that Love is? If this is true, wouldn't it be wise to stop running and start looking at our *Self* to see what needs changing *inside?*

For example, I consider being able to freely read books by all kinds of authors, on any subject of my choosing—*without fear*—a wonderful blessing. Reading has always been pleasurable to me. A fifth grade experience comes to mind. I much preferred reading and being alone to the regular classroom activities. Therefore, on many occasions after lunch, I would disappear into a vacant classroom, on the top floor of the school to finish out the day reading to my heart's content. I was amazed that the teacher never questioned where I was. I now suspect she knew what was going on but chose not to do anything about it, understanding my need.

Religious books eventually became my favorite because I was very interested in spiritual things. I was careful, however, to read only books written by members of the church I was raised in, for fear others would lead me astray. I would run—so to speak—from these other books—my fear chasing me. For years, therefore, I missed out on all the beautiful truths that were there—things which are now so joyful to me. There were events and circumstances that seemed to chase me, until I was in a corner and had to face my fear—my desire to know things being greater than my fear of reading questionable material.

My deeper fear was of maybe finding out that what I had been taught while growing up was *wrong*, which would mean everything I had grown up believing, that which provided the ground I was standing on, would crumble and I would be left standing on shifting sands. It was much easier to project *wrongness* onto the *other books*. During the process of working through this fear, I even hid the books I was reading so those around me wouldn't condemn me for reading them—revealing yet another fear—of what I perceived others would say or do. There were several books I read with fear and trembling because I knew they were *unauthorized* by the church—only to discover wherein lay the real problem. I projected the problem "out there" when in reality, it was "within." I eventually faced myself, learning to be open and able to read or hear anything without fear and without first making a judgment on it—to be more *loving*. As I did so, I was richly rewarded—discovering truths previously beyond my view. I gained new insights—understanding myself more and more. The books I feared the most became stepping stones of love on the path to discovering my true identity. And yes, I did have to rebuild with rocks when my foundation crumbled to the dust, but am grateful to be rid of the sand.

Perfect love casteth out fear. When we fear examining or contemplating another aspect of truth, we are not assured in our own convictions. Because I was not assured of my beliefs, even though I would have told you so (I had my own self fooled), fear became the teacher it took to get me to the truth. I was projecting what I didn't want to see in myself onto the church and onto others. Whether the church was guilty or not is of no importance because the only way anything could be changed for me was by looking inside myself and changing it there. It was my obligation to search things for myself and do as Paul admonished in Thessalonians, "Prove all things; hold fast that which is good."

What if we *were* to look within as we processed all that we experienced and saw "out there" and understood that it was *all* part of our Self, a reflection of our inner world? What if we were to face the enemy *within*? How would we then view what we saw; the good and bad, the right and wrong, the love and the fear? As the hot and cold illustration points out, could we know the Love that we are if we had never known anything different, like the child with temperature—if we weren't brought to an awareness of its essential elements? Would I have valued being able to search for and find truth for myself had I not experienced a feeling of being restricted to established beliefs? As I see it, experiencing opposites is the way we have of coming to *consciously* know ourselves—the Love that we are—to knowing God.

In Matthew 5:44-45, Jesus says, "Love your enemies, bless them that curse you, do good to them that hate you, and pray for them which despitefully use you, and persecute you; that ye may be the children of your Father which is in heaven." What if we were to take this advice to heart, loving and embracing not only the enemies "out there," but even the "enemy within," knowing now that without that inner and outer enemy, we would never have known the true essence of our being? Would the adversary then be bound? Does the enemy truly have any power over us when we love and forgive him/her?

In many cases, there are perceived enemies because of the physical control they have exerted over our bodies. In these situations, however, others *only* have power over the essence of who we truly are as we allow ourselves to feel negative feelings about what they have done.

They may be able to hurt the body, but no one has control over the essence of who you really are, the part of you that is eternal. You make the calls—you decide how you will react in any given situation. All experiences are God's way of helping you return to the Love that you are—to your sacred heart! The more difficult your physical or emotional challenges are, the more opportunity there is to exercise your Self in being Love. Christ was the ultimate example of this as He suffered all He did, never deviating once from His love.

Yes, *acknowledging the enemy as our own is the beginning*

of being released from his/her power and finding his/her constructive side.

With a greater understanding of what we have unknowingly imposed upon ourselves, we now have two choices. We can

1) Get in touch with our unconsciousness, remove the mask, and graciously accept all parts (counterfeit or otherwise) of our total *Self*, then bring back into our conscious awareness our true personality. Or . . .

2) Continue separating ourselves, thus perpetuating the misery of being unaware of our true identity—of our True *Self*.

We cannot change something until we know what needs to be changed. Now recognizing there is such a thing as the enemy within, we can appreciate the necessity—although we may not like it—of having *conscious* self-acceptance of that part of us. This acceptance may include parts of our personality that seem inferior or even devilish. We may even need to accept a part of us that would not, and could not, fit into the image prescribed for us by others.

Nevertheless, let it be all right if others experience some discomfort as you seek to bring about these desired changes in your *Self*. Be prepared that others (friends and family perhaps) may give you flack. Seeing your growth and the resulting changes may bring up their own issues, which they may not be ready for. By discounting your efforts, they assure themselves that self-examination is not worth pursuing. For this reason, unless they are on a similar spiritual path, they may have trouble being supportive. They may even unconsciously sabotage you out of their fear of having to look at their own stuff.

Remember, the role of actor or slave has served its purpose in your life. If your goal is to relinquish this role, you can do it simply by acknowledging the parts of your *Self* that you dislike. Doing so will be one of your greatest achievements. This doesn't mean you are a bad person or that you need to feel guilty or less-than. Accept, embrace, love and re-connect with that which you dislike in your Self. By doing so you can become the author and the master of your life. You can move on. This time, however, *you* will govern your inner enemy instead of it governing you. At last, you have a choice! Recall when you didn't know your inner enemy even existed and, as a result, you were helpless to do anything about it.

Be aware also, that by identifying and owning the less than glorious parts of your *Self*, you have the opportunity of emerging from the nonsense your undesirable choices/mistakes have created. You have the opportunity of discovering who you truly are.

If, at this juncture, we choose to disregard looking at, owning, and resolving unfinished business, we will continue to live only a portion of our life. We will miss the purpose of our journey in this realm of existence. We will miss the joy of discovering and re-claiming who we really are—our true identity, our Divine Self.

Several years ago, someone handed me a piece of paper with the following quote from a talk by Dr. Lael J. Woodbury. It spoke to my heart and has been a beacon for me and many other people since then.

> Equally complete now is each of our lives before the Lord. We explore them sequentially because we are time-

blind. But the Lord, perceiving time as space, sees us as we are, not as we are becoming. We are, for Him, beings without time. We are continually before Him—the totality of our psyches, personalities, bodies, choices, and behaviors.

If this is so—knowledge of this fact should change our entire approach to life. For life becomes, then, not a cumulative, additive process, one in which we layer on increments of perfection like successive coats of lacquer. Life is rather a challenge to discover who we are, not to determine who we shall become. Who were we, and what were we when we shouted for joy as the foundations of the earth were laid? What feats did we perform in the great battle in heaven? [. . .] In what way are we created in the image of God? The greater prophecy is not what we shall become, but what we are. The challenge is not to add on perfection, but to strip away blindness and corruption and to discover what [and who] we are. The essence is greater than the promise. We are better subsumed [occupied] in Being than we are in becoming.

If Dr. Woodbury's observations are correct, it seems we may have mis-understood, to some degree, what we are all about. To not feel forever concerned about "becoming" something unattainable bestows hope for those who may have lost hope in the race of life. We all have unknowingly allowed blindness and corruption, as Dr. Woodbury defines it, to intervene and overlay our DNA. Might any of this have a connection to our inner enemy?

There will be those of you who have already discovered your inner enemy and removed the mask. I commend you who are accepting the authenticity of the individual that you actually are. What an exciting journey of self-discovery as you continue uncovering the Truth of your Be-ing! Keep in mind that it's a process, not a pill.

Undoubtedly, our inner enemy has been a contributor to our blindness and corruption. Now knowing what needs to be changed, we can experience an exceptionally meaningful metamorphosis. Whatever we feared or felt disdain for in ourselves, we can now embrace as a teacher or friend that is absolutely essential for our wholeness.

By being accountable for our undesirable feelings, thoughts, attitudes, and behavior—by Scripting them— replacing the negative with positive feelings, we are redeeming the enemy within. We are liberating that part of our Self. We are stripping away the blindness and corruption. What a process for discovering, healing, and bringing together our whole and True Self, for restoring the Love that we are!

The good news: the inner enemy is transformed into a useful part of our personality through our conscious recognition and acceptance of it as a legitimate part of our *Self.* It complements us rather than contradicts us. What before seemed only negative now reveals a beautiful, positive side.

Redeeming the enemy within takes great spiritual courage. By accessing this courage, however, we overcome the internal conflicts we may be experiencing and return to the road of choice. We leave the detour behind. By steering our agency back to the main road we have a higher probability of discovering our True *Self,* which can only be found on this road.

Accomplishing the changes we have been discussing requires several major shifts in *Self* awareness. Some may wonder if they care to make the necessary effort in order to create these shifts. Be assured, the results are very much worth the effort required. In fact, creating the changes becomes effortless when a person gets used to the process.

When we give ourselves permission to explore and allow these new possibilities in our lives, we eventually notice it's much easier to truly love, appreciate, and embrace the Truth of our Be-ing. It is at this point—loving and accepting our *Self*—that we can genuinely love and accept others. Doing so is not a matter of achieving some impossible saint-like condition, but of being fulfilled as the person we are inherently created to *Be*.

When the inner enemy is eliminated, you become the whole person you were meant to be. You become a more congruent human Be-ing. Wholeness comes by

1) Giving your Self permission to have flaws—letting it be all right that you do have them
2) Having the fortitude to admit you've been wrong about something
3) Developing the courage to make changes as they are needed
4) Examining your incorrect perceptions and correcting them to the best of your ability
5) Facing your inner enemy head on
6) Resolving undesirable feelings, thoughts, attitudes, behaviors.

OWN IT ALL! It is *so* freeing! Whatever you learn about your *Self*, let it be all right. Often, what you consider as faults and failures have contributed to the development of your highest potential and greatest capacity for love.

When we can admit and allow our own faults and failures, we are not so quick to judge or condemn another. Many of us try to bring other people down by pointing out their failings. This is just another unconscious attempt to project our inner enemy outward. As we allow our *Self* to have flaws, we feel a stronger sense of compassion—an attribute that strengthens and lifts humankind.

Are we now primed for resolving the feelings and thoughts that don't contribute to the qualities we desire to embody? It's very important to realize, while in the process, that these conditions did not materialize overnight; therefore, they are not going to leave overnight! Remember . . . it's not a pill. It's a process. It's a journey. It may take a while to reach that blissful shore.

You may get stuck for periods of time, as I did. If you find your feelings or attitudes are not changing the way you would like, just keep on keepin' on. While you are processing, your negative qualities are becoming positive qualities; each time you Script, you are compounding light and truth and God's peace and love in your energy fields. That is exciting!

People have asked me how many times a person has to process or Script for a particular feeling, attitude, or belief. My answer is a question: How deep are the layers? We don't know how long it will take. Also, if you are not experiencing the change you desire, you may consider adjusting your verbiage a bit. If the feeling isn't being accurately identified in the way you have been stating it, you may find it more difficult to resolve. That's why it is so important to listen to your words, thoughts, and feelings. Experiment with different verbiage until you feel the desired shift.

Several improvements have been discovered since the *Script* was first introduced. These include

1) Looking into your eyes in the mirror while Scripting as often as possible

2) Scripting the same feeling 21 days in succession to change a particular pattern in your DNA

We *can* rid our *Self* of the inner enemy. We *can* be totally congruent in everything we feel, think, say, and do. Yes! Let us relinquish the self-imposed bondage we've experienced through our own unconsciousness. Let's "turn on the lights" as we travel our road of life so we can truly see where we are going.

CHAPTER 11

Can You "Let Go"?

Yielding is an action of the heart.

Now, can we let go of judging others? Can we let go of judging ourselves? Why are we told in the holy books not to judge? Scripture is full of passages on judging:

> Judge not, that ye be not judged. For with what judgement ye judge, ye shall be judged: and with what measure ye mete, it shall be measured to you again (Matthew 7:1-2). Judge not, and ye shall not be judged: condemn not, and ye shall not be condemned: forgive, and ye shall be forgiven (Luke 6:37). Let us not therefore judge one another any more: but judge this rather, that no man put a stumbling block or an occasion to fall in his brother's way (Romans 14:13). Yea, and why even of yourselves judge ye not what is right? (Luke 12:57).

Could it be that when we judge others we condemn ourselves at the same time? And isn't our judgment of someone else often final? In our mind, do we allow that person a chance to make amends or change? By judging, aren't we drawing a conclusion? And how often do we arrive at a virtuous, just, fair, or unbiased conclusion? It seems to be our unconscious nature to automatically put people into slots and categorize them as we pass judgement. When we judge, how often are we holding ourselves above the other person? Think about it. . . . The sad part of this scenario is that we never ever have all the facts! So how can we truly judge? When we feel tempted to judge, we would do better to pray for the person instead.

Here is a story that, indeed, illustrates the folly of judging.

A church was in need of a pastor. One of the elders was interested in knowing just what kind of a minister they desired. He therefore wrote a letter, as if he had received it from an applicant. He read this letter before the pulpit committee:

Gentlemen:

Understanding that your pulpit is vacant, I should like to apply for the position. I have many qualifications that I think you would appreciate. I have been blessed to preach with power and have had some success as a writer. Some say that I am a good organizer. I have been a leader in most places I have gone.

Some folks, however, have some things against me. I am over fifty years of age. I have never preached in one place for more than three years at a time. In some places I had to leave town, after my work caused riots and disturbances. I have to admit that I have been in a jail three of four times but not because of any real wrong doing. My health is not too good, though I still get a good deal done. I have had to work at my trade to help pay my way. The churches I have preached in have been small, though located in several large cities.

I have not gotten along too well with the religious leaders in different towns where I have preached. In fact, some of them have threatened me, taken me to court and even attacked me physically.

I am not too good at keeping records. I have even been known to forget those I have baptized. However, if you can use me I shall do my best for you, even if I have to work to help with my support.

The elder read this letter to the committee and asked them if they were interested in the applicant. They replied that he would never do for their church. They were not interested in any unhealthy, contentious, trouble-making, absent-minded, ex-jailbird; in fact, they felt insulted that his application had been presented.

The committee then asked the name of the applicant, whereupon the elder answered, "THE APOSTLE PAUL."

How many of us would feel as the pulpit committee did? Would we be guilty of this same judgment? How prevalent is unrighteous judgment in our society today?

The reaction to the minister's application truly gives us something to think about. Did the committee have all the facts? Do any of us ever have all the facts? Even in judging ourselves, is it possible to remember all the facts from the beginning?

As has been mentioned, when we judge others it's usually because we see in the other person that which we dislike in our *Self.* Our rejection of the person we are judging is based, ultimately, upon a rejection of something in our *Self,* of which we are not consciously aware. Whatever it is we dislike reflects our own inner enemy—of whom, thankfully, we are now aware. Judgment can also be spawned from jealousy or silent feelings of inadequacy. Often we don't recognize this within our *Self*. We may think we are simply offering our observation or opinion of another person. However, if we become emotional or reactive while doing so, it is a sure indicator we have an energy charge associated with that opinion and, therefore, some feelings that need to be resolved.

When we judge we "shoot our *Self* in the foot," for it weakens the body. It's like telling God he doesn't know what He's doing. When we judge and act without mercy we also jeopardize our Spirit, as doing this lowers our vibrations.

We judge others by their actions, yet *we* would like to be judged by our intentions. Have you ever had your intention mis-construed? Oh, that others could see our heart—our true intent—and that we could look at the heart of another instead of looking at the outward appearance. In 1 Samuel 16:7 we are reminded, "for the LORD seeth not as man seeth; for man looketh on the outward appearance, but the LORD looketh on the heart."

Judgment is usually an unconscious act. This is why our judgment of others always returns to us. In judging them we are, in effect, judging ourselves. When we feel or think negatively about someone, the subtle energy of these feelings and thoughts is naturally directed to the person. If that person unconsciously refuses to accept or receive the subtle energy we have just created, it has to go somewhere. Guess where? It's Returned to Sender. Just as we will surely become ill if we take poison into our body, so will we surely incur inner judgment if we stand in judgment of others. How would it be if, instead, we sent out healing feelings and thoughts of love to that person?

Have you ever heard of the "echo" effect? The following story perfectly illustrates this principle.

A son and his father were hiking in the mountains. Suddenly the son falls, hurts himself and screams, "AAAhhhhhhhhhhhhhh!!" To his surprise he hears a voice repeating, somewhere in the mountain, "AAAhhhhhhhhhhhhhh!!" Curious, he yells, "Who are you?" He receives the answer, "Who are you?" Angered at the response, he screams, "Coward!" He receives the answer, "Coward!"

He looks to his father and asks, "What's going on?" The father smiles and says, "My son, pay attention."

The father then screams to the mountain, "I admire you!"

The voice answers, "I admire you!"

Again the man screams, "You are a champion!"

The voice answers, "You are a champion!"

The boy is surprised, but does not understand. Then the father explains: "People call this ECHO, but really this is LIFE. It gives you back everything you say or do. Our life is simply a reflection of our actions. If you want more love in the world, create more love in your heart. If you want more competence in your team, improve your competence. This relationship applies to everything, in all aspects of life. Life will give you back everything you have given to it. If you want others to be happy, practice compassion. If you want to be happy, practice compassion.

"YOUR LIFE IS NOT A COINCIDENCE, IT'S A REFLECTION OF YOU!"

—Unknown

This is the key to all true healing—whether of body, mind, emotion, or spirit. All you truly give with emotion, you receive back compounded, including the positive. The positive, harmonious feelings and thoughts you send out and the gifts you give are only a blessing if you willingly give from your heart, blessing the gift with your love. By doing so, you immediately make a pathway by which your own healing comes to you. In other words, that which we pronounce upon someone else, we pronounce upon our *Self* at the same time.

A story that I particularly appreciate is told by a young woman.

I am a mother of three children ages 14, 12, and 3 and have recently completed my college degree. The last class I had to take was Sociology. The teacher was absolutely inspiring, with the qualities that I wish every human being had been graced. Her last project of the term was called "Smile." The class was asked to go out and smile at three people and document their reaction. I am a very friendly person and always smile at everyone and say hello anyway—so I thought this would be a piece of cake.

Soon after we were assigned the project, my husband, youngest son, and I went out to McDonalds one crisp March morning. It was just our way of sharing special play time with our son. We were standing in line, waiting to be served, when all of a sudden everyone around us began to back away, and then even my husband did. I did not move an inch. An overwhelming feeling of panic welled up inside of me as I turned to see why they had moved. As I turned around I smelled a horrible, dirty body smell, and there standing behind me were two poor homeless men. As I looked down at the short gentleman close to me, he was smiling. His beautiful sky-blue eyes were full of God's Light as he searched for acceptance. He said, "Good day" as he counted the few coins he had been clutching. The second man fumbled with his hands as he stood behind his friend. I realized the second man was mentally deficient and the blue-eyed gentleman was his salvation. I held my tears as I stood there with them. The young lady at the counter asked him what they wanted. He said, "Coffee is all, Miss" because that was all they could afford, but to sit in the restaurant and warm up, they had to buy something. They just wanted to be warm. Then I really felt it . . . the compulsion was so great I almost reached out and embraced the little man with the blue eyes. That is when I noticed all eyes in the restaurant were set on me—judging my every action. I smiled and asked the young lady behind the counter to give me two more breakfast meals on a separate tray. I then walked around the corner to the table the men had chosen as a resting spot. I put the tray on the table and laid my hand on the blue-eyed gentleman's cold hand. He looked up at me, with tears in his eyes, and said, "Thank you." I leaned over, began to pat his hand and said, "I did not do this [just] for you—God is here working through me to give you hope." I started to cry as I walked away to join my husband and son. When I sat down my husband smiled at me and said, "That is why God gave you to me, honey—to give me hope." We held hands for a moment, and at that time we knew that only because of the Grace that we had been given, were we able to give.

We are not church goers, but we are believers. That day showed me the pure Light of God's sweet love. I returned to college on the last evening of class with this story in hand. I turned in my project and the instructor read it . . . then she looked up at me and said, "May I share this?" I slowly nodded as she got the attention of the class. She began to read, and that is when I knew that we, as human beings and being part of God, share this need to heal people and to be healed. In my own way I had touched the people at McDonalds, my husband, son, instructor, and every soul that shared the classroom on the last night I spent as a college student. I graduated with one of the biggest lessons I would ever learn . . . UNCONDITIONAL ACCEPTANCE.

You will recall that when you hate and fear something in yourself, it will appear dreadful and evil; but if you accept it, the fearfulness will disappear. Yes, there is evil on the earth, but evil is of man's own doing and choosing. Evil was not created by, nor is it a part of, God. Evil is man's creation. In fact, the word evil reversed is God's desire for you—l-i-v-e—that you live the Love you are. By stripping evil of its power and turning it around—you live!

I've always loved this quote from Shakespeare, and it seems appropriate here: "This above all; to thine own self be true and it must follow, as night the day, Thou canst not then be false to any man." Truer words were never spoken! When you are true to your *Self*, others automatically trust you, and they don't even know or understand why.

It would be well to observe that there is a difference between judging and evaluating a situation or person. Discerning the circumstances before getting involved is always a wise and good practice. Naturally we need to exercise discernment as to a person's honesty and integrity. In making decisions or choices, it is important to ascertain whether a situation will be for our good or not.

Yes, we are very often called upon to make value

judgments in our day-to-day decisions. Be aware! There is a fine line between discerning and judging. Judgment takes you out of peace whereas discernment provides you awareness without emotional involvement. It *is* necessary for us to exercise constant awareness and wisdom. Let us not confuse discernment with judgment and thereby avoid censuring someone erroneously.

Continually pray for the power of discernment—for insight, for wisdom, for compassion. Pray for the ability to let go of blame and judgment and to come from love and understanding. (If ye ask not, ye receive not.)

The vital thing to remember is there is *no* way we can pass judgment on another person without error! There is *no* way we can fully and accurately see things through someone else's eyes. There is *no* way we can know what another person's experiences and up-bringing have brought to their life.

Each of us was conceived under distinctive circumstances. Each of us has experienced an entirely individual incubation period, birth, and childhood. Each of us has uniquely different parents. Each of us experiences a totally divergent range of input. And each of us has had singular histories that have caused us to be who we are (to say nothing of what we've inherited in our DNA!) Therefore, why would we think we could stand in another's shoes and know what makes them tick? Only God knows the intent of a person's heart.

Perhaps we now understand with more compassion that each of us is traveling our own road in life. Nevertheless, we are each striving to reach the same destination—home. Despite what some may think, no one person has all the answers! Each of us has unknowingly designed our own distinct and unique experiences for our individual development. Even though we may not fully grasp our own importance, each of us is as important as the other. Each of us is an individual, brilliant thread in God's resplendent tapestry, and it takes all of us to complete that tapestry. Therefore, we would do well to honor our fellow travelers on their journey through life by allowing them their own experiences without involving our energy.

CHAPTER 12

Brent's Story

It's only through the heart that one can see clearly.
—Glenda Green

I would like to share an experience I had with a young man who truly helped me understand the non-judging principle. In 1993, while living in Las Vegas, Nevada, I received a desperate telephone call from an anguished mother in a neighboring state. She wanted to know if I ever worked with people suffering from AIDS. We talked awhile, and she told me the story of her 36-year-old son, Brent.

In third grade he developed a urinary tract condition that required the attention of a specialist. They lived in a small town which necessitated their traveling many miles to the city every six months, for his treatments. This continued until Brent was a junior in high school, at which point he bravely told his ecclesiastical leader that the doctor had been sexually molesting him for all those years. Naturally, as a boy he didn't know or understand what constituted treatment for his urinary tract problem. "If you can't trust your doctor, who can you trust?" was the premise in those days. I don't know how long Brent had battled with what was happening in the doctor's office, but at some point he finally realized the inappropriateness of the doctor's "treatments" and couldn't tolerate them any longer.

Being free of treatments was wonderful, but those treatments had set the stage for a much greater drama in Brent's life. He shared with me how for several years he fought against being attracted to other men. Eventually, at age 23 he could fight it no longer. He moved to California where he would be free to live as he chose without being ostracized by the community, and there he became a legal secretary.

When Brent came to see me (at his own choosing), his AIDS was well advanced. His companion had just left him, so he was not only suffering from the ravages of AIDS but from feelings of rejection and abandonment. Brent was deeply discouraged and depressed. I could see that this hurting child of God had lost all hope of any happiness in his life. Before we got into the matter at hand, we established a relationship of trust. He could tell that I sincerely cared about him and his plight—not only the AIDS but also his devastation at being left alone.

In working with people, I always begin by reviewing how the laws of the universe work, starting with the simple and moving into more complex natural laws. Brent couldn't connect with anything I said. He just kept saying, "That may be how you understand it, but I don't agree." He couldn't accept that there was a God, or a higher source, or even universal laws. I did my best to find some point of reference with which he could identify, but he continued to disagree. Even so we were able to examine his feelings, deal with some of his frustrations, and then do some processing.

When Brent returned the next day, I was with a client on the phone, so I invited him to make himself at home while I finished my conversation in my office. A few minutes later I heard the song "If I Loved You" from the musical *Carousel* being played, oh so beautifully, on the piano. My thought was, I must have that arrangement! It's the most beautiful rendition of "If I Loved You" I've ever heard! Brent was playing with more sensitivity than I'd heard in a long time (and I taught piano for 43 years). I completed my conversation before he finished playing the piece, so I lingered in my office until he finished. I then went into the living room and complimented him on his playing. I could hardly wait to learn the name of the arranger so that I could purchase the piece and learn it. When I asked Brent who the arranger was, he looked quite surprised and simply said, "Me." Much to my disappointment, he had never written it out.

It was obvious that Brent had a beautiful gift. I inquired how much time he spent at the piano. He indicated that he hardly played anymore. I understood first hand the therapeutic benefits of playing the piano. And due to the sensitive nature of his gift, I knew he would truly benefit from spending more time at the piano, so I encouraged him to return to playing more often.

After three sessions Brent returned to California. I had no idea if he felt we'd accomplished anything. Nevertheless, we kept in touch. About two months later I had occasion to visit southern California. I phoned Brent to ask if he would like to meet with me; I had thought of some new possibilities for helping him. He agreed to meet.

We spent a fruitful afternoon working on the emotional causes of his AIDS and looking a little deeper into his heart.

I felt extremely good about what we accomplished. Since the particular therapy I used had always rendered very satisfying results with other people, I felt hopeful that our session that afternoon would produce some changes in his blood chemistry. He promised to let me know the results of his next blood test.

As I bade him farewell and drove away, encouraged by all the processing we had done, I was suddenly overwhelmed with the feeling that Brent was not through with this journey yet—that he still had many miles to go and much to learn before this phase of his life would be complete. I knew his blood work would not change. Even though I didn't understand what it was Brent had come to accomplish through these particular challenges, I knew it was all "perfect." Not only was he going to gain the insights he needed, but by staying on this particular path, he would also be teaching many others that which they needed to learn. Rather than inform Brent of what I had come to understand, I decided to wait until I heard from him.

Interestingly, I received a letter from Brent three weeks later. He informed me that his blood hadn't changed. "What do I do now, coach?" he asked. What could I say? My greatest desire was to be supportive and to let him know I cared. In my reply, I expressed disappointment that his blood work hadn't shown improvement. I explained that after driving away on the day we worked together, I suddenly experienced a knowing that his blood would not improve. I affirmed my love and concern and assured him of my continued support.

We kept in touch. Brent would write or call, as would I. He shared with me the contributions he was making to society and the changes that were taking place in his life. He told me about interesting new people he was meeting, what he was learning from them, and how they were contributing to his life. (I later learned how much he gave of himself and contributed to others, as well.) About a year after our first meeting, Brent called and told me that God was once again part of his life. There was hope for a brighter tomorrow!

Shortly after this time, my family relocated. Later, when I phoned Brent to let him know of our move, he was no longer at his old number. Even though my prayers were with him and I thought about him often, we never reconnected.

More than two years went by. One day in the Spring of 1996, I was at a meeting in a large metropolitan city. During a break, I was talking to friends when I felt someone slip their arm around my waist. I quickly glanced over to see who it was. There was a woman about my age whom I had never met before. And yet I *knew* that I knew her. She waited until I finished my conversation, and as I turned to speak to her, I must have looked puzzled, for she said, "I'm Brent's mother."

I immediately hugged her and asked about Brent. She told me that he was gone; he had died a year earlier. She shared with me what had transpired after I lost contact with him. Brent's mother and father had moved to California and into an apartment with Brent three months before he died. She told me of all the beautiful experiences they'd had with him during that time; of the wonderful healing that had taken place between Brent and his father and others in the family. Our tears flowed as we talked. I felt as if I had known her all my life. We lost track of time as we talked.

Soon the meeting resumed, but before we said good-bye she asked if I would like an audio tape of Brent's piano music he had recorded two weeks before his passing. Of course my answer was, "Yes!"

A few of Brent's friends had pooled their resources and hired a studio for him to record his music. They were desirous that his memory live on for those who loved to hear him play. Before we left the meeting, Brent's mother brought me one of those tapes.

Shortly after my husband and I started our five-hour drive home, we began listening to the tape. Well, the first piece Brent played was "If I Loved You." Of course, that reduced me to tears as I thought about the first time I heard him play. My thought was, Oh, I'll quit crying when he finishes this. I was wrong! The next song was "Somewhere My Love," then "Shenandoah," "You'll Never Walk Alone," "No Other Love" (from Chopin's Etude), "The Rose," "Music of the Night," "Somewhere Over the Rainbow," "Somewhere in Time," "The Way We Were," "Silent Night,"—and on and on. There were also hymns from the church of his youth interspersed throughout the tape. All of these pieces were very special to me and my husband because either I played them or he sang them.

We both felt the depth of Brent's soul as we listened to his music. The most remarkable sound I heard in his beautiful renditions, however, was the healing that had taken place in this young man's heart. That he had found God again was truly obvious, and that he had found himself was unquestionable.

My husband was as deeply affected by Brent's music as I was. He almost had to pull the car to the side of the road because of his tears. Even though we are a family of musicians, I've never heard anything more poignant or that touched my heart as much as Brent's playing. As we continued listening to the music during the next hour, my repeated thought was, This young man's story must be told!

I was so filled with emotion—knowing how wracked his soul was upon first meeting him and realizing the distance he had come since then—that I waited several weeks before letting Brent's mother know how his music had affected us. When I did finally talk to her I learned more about Brent's life. It was very touching, and again I was convinced that someone ought to tell his story.

From his music it was obvious that Brent had not only found himself but had re-established his relationship with his Creator. Before he died, Brent told his mother that he knew—and he knew that she knew—that he had at some level, somewhere, sometime chosen to travel this particular journey. He knew it was for the purpose of learning what he needed to learn to heal from his heart and re-connect with his Maker.

How can I explain the way this experience touched my life? I can't. You would have to have known Brent to feel the exquisiteness of his healing. All I can tell you is that during the next year, I played his music many, many times and shared it with countless others, providing a little background on Brent as they listened. Many felt as if they had known him, too.

Each time I heard the music I was strengthened and reminded of the goodness life offers as we choose finding our Truth and seeking Him.

As time went on and I became involved in working with people, taking care of my responsibilities, and writing this book, Brent's music was given a rest for a while. Then in August of 1997, I was driving across northern Arizona by myself and decided to listen to Brent's tape. As the notes of his beautiful music filled the car, I found myself responding to it as if I were hearing it for the first time! Once again, his renditions reached right into the depths of my soul. Now this is ridiculous, I thought. You've heard this music many times. Why are you still reacting this way? I kept asking myself that question. Then, as before, I felt this young man's story must be told.

I resolved to call Brent's mother after I returned home. I wanted to spend time learning all the details of his life. I would write Brent's story myself. Yes, I thought, I must get all the details! Then all of a sudden I heard, oh, so softly, "It doesn't matter. The details do not matter. What matters is that Brent re-connected with his Maker."

Why of course! The importance of knowing Brent in my life was to show me that the details were and are insignificant; that it doesn't matter the path someone trods or how they finally come to know their Truth. What did matter was that Brent faced his dragons. He did much soul-searching. He took responsibility and became accountable for his life. He arrived at a better understanding and knowledge of himself. He healed his relationships, and re-established his connection with his Father in Heaven.

Just how important is it for each of us to accomplish this? And does it make any difference how we do it? We are all traveling a different road. Your journey is not the same as mine, nor is mine the same as yours or anyone else's. The differences don't matter, as long as we reach the same destination.

Regardless of our individual journeys, we all experience challenges—we all have mountains to climb and rivers to cross. Just because we don't all arrive at our designated destination at the same time or in the same way doesn't mean one way is better than another, or that your way is better than mine, or mine is better than yours. Each way is just different! And it's okay. There are many roads to home.

Recently I saw a bumper sticker that said, Stop Hate Crimes! Honor diversity. My reaction to this gem of a message was, yes!

I couldn't help but wonder: Do we feel (notice, I didn't say *think*, because *hate* is a feeling, and has many appendages) that everyone ought to conform to our way of feeling, thinking, seeing, and doing things? Do we feel that if others don't agree with our way, something is wrong with them?

A recent letter to "Dear Abby" says it all: " . . . Whenever I hear about intolerance, I'm reminded of an old poem. (I do not know the author.) It made me think. Perhaps it will touch one of your other readers as well." George R. Goldie IV, Oxnard, California.

THE COLD WITHIN

Six humans trapped in happenstance
In dark and bitter cold,
Each one possessed a stick of wood,
Or so the story's told.
Their dying fire in need of logs
The first woman held hers back,

For of the faces around the fire,
She noticed one was black.
The next man looking across the way
Saw not one of his church,
And couldn't bring himself to give
The fire his stick of birch.
The third one sat in tattered clothes
He gave his coat a hitch,
Why should his log be put to use,
To warm the idle rich?
The rich man just sat back and thought
Of the wealth he had in store,
And how to keep what he had earned,
From the lazy, shiftless poor.
The black man's face bespoke revenge
As the fire passed from sight,
For all he saw in his stick of wood
Was a chance to spite the white.
The last man of this forlorn group
Did naught except for gain,
Giving only to those who gave,
Was how he played the game.
The logs held tight in death's still hands
Was proof of human sin,
They didn't die from the cold without,
They died from the cold within.

Hasn't this attitude contributed to dictatorships and human bondage in the past? Can't this attitude also encourage some to deprive others of their free choice, free will, or free agency? Part of the uniqueness of life is the diversity in each of us! Even the first law of Art is "contrast." Steven R. Covey, author of "Seven Habits of Highly Successful

People," suggests that we "rejoice in our differences!"

Besides honoring each other's inherent diversity, each of us need to honor our own diversity, our own uniqueness, our own individuality. Remember that every person has been traveling a different path than you. Their journey has taken them through entirely different scenery than yours. Why think or feel that someone is stupid or crazy if they don't see things the way you do? What happened to tolerance, acceptance, and allowance? Where did the false idea begin that we should all feel and think the same, anyway?

Somewhere, sometime, an underlying cultural belief must have been established and perpetuated. Did the belief have to do with everyone feeling and thinking alike, acting alike, and looking alike? Did the belief indicate that if we didn't fall into line with everyone else, obviously there must be something wrong with us? If we were the one in error were we then labeled as different, strange, or flawed.

Who came up with the original misconception or idea that we *must* be separate from each other? Can you see the adversarial influences in this mind set? Is it this influence that needs a basis for conflict; that would have us magnify our differences? For if we aren't separate from each other, how can we prove that we are better? How can we create chaos? How can we have wars? Wait a minute! There is definitely something absurd about this picture. Don't we all share the same needs, the same feelings, desires, hopes, and dreams?

In ways that we might not fully comprehend, we are all connected and part of the whole. How sad that we so often feel separate and apart from others—especially in our un-consciousness, in our un-awareness. But, by looking at—

not past—each person we see, we recognize that no matter what language they speak or from which country or culture they originate; no matter how they live, they all desire the same things in life that we desire.

Don't they love their children just as we love ours? Don't they grieve when a loved one dies, just as we do? Don't they rejoice when a loved one gets married or has a new baby, the same as we do? They have experienced pain, hurt, disappointment, sorrow, and suffering too. Don't we all have the same heart's desire? Don't we all long for acceptance, belonging, and happiness, to be valued, appreciated, and loved?

Instead of just looking, instead of just listening, we must completely open our eyes, our ears and our hearts. Then we will we see, hear, and truly feel these universal human needs in every individual we meet. We will then know that we, indeed, have much in common with all of humankind— regardless of ethnic background, color, or creed; regardless of beliefs, handicaps, or misfortunes; regardless of glory, fame, or success.

If you have had a difficult time overcoming judgment and blame, perhaps Scripting will resolve these tendencies. Know that it's one thing to be an observer and point out everything that's wrong with other people and the world, but it's quite another to step down from the spectator's seat and—instead of just observing—become a participant. By participating you more readily see things that are right with the world. You begin contributing to the solution of the problems, rather than being part of them. (Remember the old song, "Let there be peace on earth—and let it begin with me?")

Ask your Spirit/Super-Conscious/Higher-Self to locate the origin of the feelings that have caused you to blame others and to be judgmental. The positive replacement could be, "I choose Be-ing loving and understanding of myself and others; I feel loving and understanding of myself and others; I am loving and understanding of myself and others. I realize we are all on our own, unparalleled journey. Therefore, even if I don't agree with what someone is doing or saying, I allow them their own experiences and their own journey without judgment or blame. I choose accepting them just the way they are. I feel unconditional acceptance of everyone. I am accepting all God's children, exactly as they are."

CHAPTER 13

Allowing All of Life

Outer reforms are useless unless the inner state is changed.

—Unknown

Now that you are no longer a participant in the blaming and judging game, the next question is, Are you truly accepting of others? Do you have a challenge accepting anyone just as they are, loving them and sincerely valuing them, regardless of their apparent or perceived shortcomings?

As parents, sometimes we can be relentless in our efforts to make our children perfect. Why? Is our motivation unconscious? Let's honestly examine our intent. Is it because we want our children to be acceptable in society? Or do we believe that the better they are the more acceptable we are? Could the faults we see in our children remind us of the ones we dislike in ourselves (that inner enemy)?

Perhaps we sincerely desire instilling in our off-spring love for their fellow man. We would like them to exemplify kindness, consideration, integrity, acceptance and sensitivity to others, simply because that's the formula God gave us.

How many of us accept someone only if they meet the

criteria we deem as acceptable? If so, how is this criteria established? What makes us the authority? What makes us the judge? When a person says something like: "Joe is just too quiet," or "Your hair is too tidy," or "Mary doesn't dress right," my response is, According to whom? Yes, who is the authority on someone's unacceptability—in any area of life?

Following is a story that gives us much food for thought.

The Creightons were very proud of [pleased with] their son, Frank. When he went to college, naturally they missed him; but he wrote and they looked forward to his letters and saw him on weekends. Then Frank was drafted into the army.

After he had been in the army about five months, he received his call to go to Vietnam. Of course, the parents' anxiety for his first letter was greater than ever before. And every week they heard from him and were thankful for his well-being. Then one week went by without a letter . . . two weeks . . . and finally three. At the end of the third week a telegram came, saying, "We regret to inform you that your son has been missing for three weeks and is presumed to have been killed in action while fighting for his country." The parents were shocked and grieved. They tried to accept the situation and go on living, but it was tragically lonesome without Frank.

About three weeks later, however, the phone rang. When Mrs. Creighton answered it, a voice on the other end said, "Mother, it's Frank. They found me, and I'm going to be all right. I'm in the United States and I'm coming home soon."

Mrs. Creighton was overjoyed; with tears running down her cheeks she sobbed, "Oh, that's wonderful! That's just wonderful, Frank."

There was silence for a moment, and then Frank said, "Mother, I want to ask you something that is important to me. While I've been here, I've met a lot of wonderful people and I've really become close friends with some. There is one fellow I would like to bring home with me to meet you and Dad. And I would like to know if it would be all right if he could stay and live with us, because he has no place to go."

His mother assured him it would be all right.

Then Frank said, "You see, he wasn't as lucky as some; he was injured in battle. He was hit by a blast and his face is all disfigured. He lost his leg, and his right hand is missing. So you see, he feels uneasy about how others will accept him."

Frank's mother stopped to think a minute. She began to wonder how things would work out, and what people in town would think of someone like that. She said, "Sure Frank, you bring him home—for a visit, that is. We would love to meet him and have him stay for a while; but about his staying with us permanently, well, we'll have to think about that." There was silence for a minute, and then Frank said, "Okay, Mother," and hung up.

A week went by without any word from Frank, and then a telegram arrived—"We regret to inform you that your son has taken his life. We would like you to come and identify the body."

Their wonderful son was gone! The horror stricken parents could only ask themselves, why had he done this? When they walked into the room to identify the body of their son, they found a young man with a disfigured face, one leg missing, and his right hand gone.

How stunned would you have been? Can you imagine what this mother must have felt? What anguish did she go through knowing that had she chosen a different answer for her son—had she chosen a different attitude—she might have saved his life. What a balance our words and attitudes can affect in the lives of others!

Is there any merit in leaving blame and judgement behind without Be-ing accepting, allowing, and loving? In other words, letting whatever "is" just "be."

Now is the time to determine the direction of your journey. Where are you interested in going? Carefully consider your choices. Do you like being where you are in life right now? Would you prefer more peace, freedom, joy, and love? There *are* ways of achieving a greater measure of satisfaction and moving beyond the results you have previously experienced. Place your *Self* in the driver's seat as you return to the main road on your journey through life.

Remember, the things out there are not the cause of your problems. The answers to the obstacles in your life can be found within. And it doesn't matter how those obstacles got there. If you have a question, look inside. The answer is there. There is no *outer* change until there is first an *inner* change.

As you concentrate on finding answers within, you take charge of life's challenges, problems, and negative experiences. It is your conscious and consistent effort that puts you on a new path to achieving mastery of *Self*. Epictetus wisely tells us, *"No man is free who is not master of himself."*

When we assume responsibility for our lives, we automatically do the *right* (fitting, proper or appropriate) thing for the *right* reasons. We understand that we alone are accountable for removing our mask; for trading the causes of unfavorable effects for ones that create favorable effects;

for becoming the author instead of being the actor of our life's story. Uprooting judgment and blame is a priority in our lives as we turn from our detour onto the main road. Returning to the Love that we are—the Truth of our Being—and reclaiming our God-given power is truly a worthwhile endeavor.

Remember that no matter what we have been through or experienced in life, we only hinder ourselves by holding onto inharmonious feelings from the past. We also affect the bigger picture. Even though each of us is only one person, consider the effect that is created when the energies of our hurt, hate, bitterness, fear, sorrow, anger, and resentment resonate with all the other people in the world who are experiencing the same feelings? What transpires when our negative energies combine with everyone else's? Could we eventually end up with millions—or billions—of hurting people projecting these same energies into our universe? If enough of us are suffering and everything we feel, think, say, and do is projected outward, how does this affect the world around us? Talk about chaos! Could we be contributing to the condition the world is in at present?

What is happening to us? A student from Columbine High School expressed it like this in an e-mail.

The paradox of our time in history is that we have taller
buildings, but shorter tempers;
Wider freeways, but narrower viewpoints;
We spend more, but have less;
We buy more, but enjoy it less.
We have bigger houses but smaller families;
More conveniences, but less time;

We have more degrees, but less sense;
More knowledge, but less judgment [wisdom];
More experts, but more problems;
More medicine, but less wellness.
We have multiplied our possessions, but reduced our
    values.
We talk too much, love too seldom, and hate too often.
We've learned how to make a living, but not a life;
We've added years to life, not life to years.
We've been all the way to the moon and back,
    but have trouble crossing the street to meet the new
    neighbor.
We have higher incomes, but lower morals;
More leisure, but less fun;
More kinds of food, but less nutrition.
These are days of two incomes, but more divorce;
    of fancier houses, but broken homes.
A time when technology can bring this letter to you,
    and a time when you can choose either to make a
    difference . . . or just hit "delete."

The good news is that you have the power within you to do something about the situation. You *can* make a difference. How? Start by creating an energy shift in your *Self,* bringing all the areas and aspects of your Be-ing together while returning to the main road. Remember, everything is energy, including feelings and thoughts—even memories.

By each of us doing our best to shift and change these energies, do you think we could make a difference in our family, in our community, and in our country? What about our world? I'm certain we can!

We know the deleterious effects of negative feelings. Now consider the power of positive feelings—especially forgiveness and love. Oh, that we could comprehend; if we could see, with our eyes, the far reaching effects love could bring to humankind. We would be amazed.

How many of us does it take to effect an energy shift? Have you ever heard of "Critical Mass," or perhaps a more familiar reference, "The Hundredth Monkey"? For those of you unfamiliar with these terms, here's a version of "The Hundredth Monkey" as I heard it.

Several years ago, some islands off the coast of Japan were hit by a typhoon that destroyed most of the vegetation. In order to preserve the monkey population, sweet potatoes were flown over the islands daily and dropped for the monkeys to eat. The Japanese also set up research posts to study the behavior of the monkeys during this time.

One day a little 18-month old monkey picked up her sweet potato. Instead of eating it she carried it to the water and washed off the sand. Naturally the potato was more pleasant to eat without the sand. So, this little monkey reported her findings to her mother. Of course the discovery was shared with one monkey after another. It only took one hundred monkeys washing their sweet potatoes on that first island, before the monkeys on the neighboring island started doing the same thing—en masse. In other words, the idea (the thought field) for washing the potatoes expanded with each new monkey washing its potato, until the thought bridged the two islands and all the monkeys were doing it. This is a true story. (Ken Keyes, Jr., *The Hundredth Monkey*)

It may take more than a hundred people to create an energy shift that makes a significant difference in the world, but whatever the required number, it *can* happen!

CHAPTER 14

Re-Visiting the Past

Wisdom is knowing what to do next.
Skill is knowing how to do it.
Virtue is doing it.

—Unknown

For the majority of us, our daily lives are governed by experiences and memories from the past. Most of us even live in the past without realizing it. Or, when this proves too painful, we escape into the future and pilot our lives through eyes of fantasy. We may not realize that by letting go of the past and Be-ing in the present, we allow life to flow more smoothly.

The importance of facing and resolving our buried hurts and feelings has only recently come to light. Therefore, most of us didn't know or understand that by resolving our feelings we can move out of the past and claim the present; we can proceed through life living in *present time*—living in the *now*.

For too long our collective mindset suggested there was nothing we could do about the past except feel anger, bitterness and guilt. If we talked about regrets or hurts we were likely told there was nothing we could do about them, or that we should just get over it.

True, the past is lost and gone forever, but there *is* something you can do about the negative energies that remain. Although your main concern is with the *now*—with the *present*—if you are still experiencing ghosts of the past, there *is* a way of changing these energies. There is a way for those ghosts to stop interfering with your progress and finally allow you peace. Ultimately you choose whether feelings from the past keep you in bondage behind your protective wall, or whether you transform them into a chisel and chip away the blocks that prevent you from true freedom and peace.

You have already been offered two important tools (*Scripting* and *Vocalizing*) to assist in breaking your confines and moving beyond. In this chapter I will share another beneficial tool that goes hand in hand with the Script.

As you know, everything is energy. As you also know, this energy includes the unresolved feelings buried deep inside—feelings acquired from unfavorable experiences with people, places, circumstances or events. The energies of which we speak are those that left negative imprints somewhere in your Be-ing.

In his book, *The Law and the Promise*, Neville Goddard tells us that we—each of us—and our past are one continuous structure. A structure containing all of the facts that have been saved and are still operating below the threshold of our conscious mind. For us, these facts are merely history. A history that seems unalterable, dead and firmly fixed

in the past. In actuality,
our life—now.   ts still live. They are part of

Yes, everything we have c
everything we have ever seen, thought, said, or done;
us is still registered in our DN ad or had happen to
because nothing disappears (energie mory banks. And
don't disappear), the only way of freein hange, but they
mistakes and hurts of the past is by res elves from the
transforming their energies. Everything that them—by
still exists through the energy it created. The pas ever been
and it produces—and keeps producing—its resu exists,
results materialize in various ways, but the first a nd best
indicators of what cries out for healing are inharmonious
feelings and thoughts that take us out of peace.

Neville tells us that if we are able to go back in memory,
then seek for and destroy [re-solve] the negativity, where
ever it lies, we can be liberated from the past. More often
than not, however, we don't have a conscious memory of
where the negativity began. This is why the Script is so powerful! The all-knowing part of us *does* know where our feelings and thoughts originated. We simply give our Spirit,
Super-Conscious, Universal Mind, or Higher Self the
assignment of locating the origin of the feeling or thought
that needs re-solution.

We have discussed two tools of resolution for changing
or discharging undesirable energies: *Scripting* and
Vocalizing. A third tool, *Revising*, is particularly useful
when you do have a conscious memory of where the negativity began.

Neville suggests that a healthy and productive daily
exercise is to *re-live* any negativity of the day, in your mind's

you had lived it. Revise any undesirable happening, as you conforms to the way you would have preferred it. words, experience in your imagination the revise n of your day exactly as you would have liked it to nting news. For example: suppose today's mail brings you dis onform to the news you wish you had rewriting it in your imagination read the revised letter received. over and er again. This is the essence of Revising, and it resul in *reversal* as it creates a different pathway for the old energy to travel.

Revising is of extreme importance when the intent is to change oneself, when there is a sincere desire to be something different or better. Every time one re-lives an event as they would have liked it to happen, there is the element of re-shaping one's outcome.

When a person begins revising even a portion of the problems or challenges of the day they, in effect, begin working on themselves. Every re-vision is a victory for the *Self*, a victory over the inner enemy. "A man's foes are those of his own household" (Matthew 10:36). And his household is his state of mind. Aren't most of our battles fought in our own imaginations?

Besides revising incidents within a day, you can also revise the past by going back and re-playing a scene in your mind as you would have liked it to occur initially. This revision results in reversing or changing the energy of the original scene or event.

By changing these energies of the past, you are changing your life because you *are* transforming energy. According to Neville, the causes of any unfavorable circumstances in the present are usually the unresolved scenes of the past. In other words, the past and the present form the whole structure of man. By altering the energies of the past and the present you are also altering the results of the present and the future.

Therefore, *Revising* is another worthwhile method for correcting, changing, and resolving negative or unproductive energies. You can think of it as *re-visioning*. In other words, *re-vision* something as you *re-visit* it and see it the way you would like to have seen it in the first place. If the past has created the present, so will *Re-vising* incidents of the past *re-create* the present and the future.

Revising an incident does not change the original outcome, but it does change the old imprint, the old charge of energy, and the sting of the old, unpleasant outcome. If an emotional block was created due to a certain incident in your life, Revising shifts the unfavorable energies of that incident and often removes the block. Say that you participated in a Spelling Bee as a child and misspelled a simple word. All the students probably had a good time laughing at your mistake—causing you embarrassment and humiliation. Chances are a mental block was created by that incident, and either spelling or getting up in front of a group has been one of your least favorite things to do ever since. So, revise the Spelling Bee and see a different outcome . . . until that energy has shifted.

The same would apply if you had a difficult time reading in front of your class. A block could have been created that, to this day, causes you to *sweat blood* or to *freeze* when you have to read something in front of others. Go back and revise that incident as many times as necessary. See and feel yourself in the scene flowing effortlessly through the experience with no problem. *See* yourself reading with confidence. *Feel* your confidence. *Breathe* it into your lungs.

By walking through an old unpleasant incident, re-playing it numerous times in your imagination so the outcome is the ideal, you will ultimately sense an energy shift and feel an attitude change. Do it consistently and as often as needed to establish a permanent shift.

Revising primarily creates a feeling of peace about a painful incident. This time, *you* are the author of the scene—*you* are the one in charge of the situation. *You* are the one determining the outcome. Even if much time has elapsed since the incident occurred, your internal energy has the ability to shift significantly, thereby affecting a more desirable outcome in the future. Actually, revising an incident can be very simple and quite exciting. Perhaps the biggest challenge is remaining focused while you are in the process, which is necessary for optimal effectiveness.

Many of the scenes we would like to revise may be from our childhood, and our Child aspect has been stuck there for a long time. A significant benefit of Revising is that it finally empowers the Child to do something about an incident it was helpless to do at the time it occurred, thereby empowering and maturing up that Child.

As you Re-vise, strongly consider creating the outcome in your imagination as a win-win situation for everyone concerned, recalling that *the energy you send out ultimately comes back to you*. Extend love and forgiveness to those involved. See them as your friends. Express gratitude for the experience. It was part of your schooling.

Keep in mind that we create with our thoughts and feelings and with our imagination every minute. As you mentally participate in revising, literally see the outcome you desire. See it happening in your mind's eye; feel the new feelings you desire as deeply as possible. Incorporating all your senses as you revise delivers greater results. So add smelling the outcome in your imagination (if there's anything to smell); hearing it with your mind's ear; touching it with your mind's hand; and even having a sense of tasting it. By participating in this fun process, the harmony you are seeking will eventually be yours.

Developing the ability to revise your negative experiences and thus become effective at quickly changing energies is yours for the taking. Continue revising. You will know the desired energy shift has occurred when you feel lighter and more peaceful about the issue or event the next time you reference it.

Though you are dealing with things of the past, your primary concern must be with the now—with the present—because the present is all you have available. Nevertheless, the present determines your emotional and spiritual health, and that of your family. Your future happiness is also determined in the present.

Remember that whichever method of processing you choose (Scripting, Vocalizing, Revising), it will be more effective if you stay in present time. By doing so, your ability to handle daily challenges will greatly increase.

Yes, it is the past that needs healing. But because you cannot physically go back and change the past, doing the next best thing is imperative! It *is* possible to be in the now and change an energy (still inside you) of something that was created in the past. Anyone can do it. Don't allow old history to keep you in bondage behind your wall. Let the Revising, or other tools, provide you with a chisel for dismantling the wall and setting you free.

How exciting and simple it is that recognizing, owning, and finally processing your feelings can be so liberating! Embrace those negative feelings and energies that need changing. You, and only you, are the master of your destiny! If you've ever had a desire to change your life, there's no better time than the present.

CHAPTER 15

The Crowning Principle

He who cannot forgive others, breaks the bridge
over which he himself must pass.

—William Thackery

We can implement all the tools in the world as we are Healing Feelings . . . From Our Heart, and we can use them from now until the cows come home. If, however, we leave out the most important and powerful healing principle upon the face of the earth, we are just playing "Ring around the Rosy"—fruitlessly going through the motions! By embracing this powerful principle and bringing it into our very Be-ing, we can quickly end our labor intensive chiseling of mortar between the blocks. How? This healing principle is the solvent that allows the mortar to simply dissolve, so that the blocks effortlessly fall away.

What is this powerful healing principle? *Forgiveness!* Simply, forgiving. . . .

How can we heal from our heart and Be the Love that we are if we don't forgive? What does forgiveness really mean? Noah Webster's 1828 *Dictionary of the English*

Language defines forgive as: "To pardon; to remit, as an offense or debt; to overlook an offense, and treat the offender as not guilty." *Forgiveness* is defined as "The act of forgiving; the pardon of an offender, by which he is considered and treated as not guilty."

Why is it essential for us to forgive? Do we forgive for our own benefit, or for the benefit of others? William Thackeray once said, "He who cannot forgive others, breaks the bridge over which he himself must pass."

Joan Borysenko, Ph.D., foremost authority on mind/body medicine and author of nine books on spirituality and healing, shares her knowing with us. Her experiences with patients has taught her the importance of learning the art and practice of forgiveness for healing. She tells us that when you are in judgment of yourself, you cannot be in the present moment and you experience constant stress. If your happiness depends on receiving an apology from someone who has hurt you, you have given someone else power over your well-being. The best solution is to forgive them.

By not forgiving yourself or others, you will eventually build up feelings of anger, helplessness, cynicism, and depression. Again, Joan Borysenko tells us, "Helplessness and victimization have been linked to poor immune system function, while cynicism and anger have been linked to high blood pressure, high cholesterol, and increased risk of coronary disease."

Yes, forgiveness has to do with you, not the other person, although the other person clearly benefits as well. Forgiveness can only come from within—from the heart. By letting go of any pride or resentment that may be standing in your way, and forgiving totally from your heart, the very deepest healing can occur. Each time you forgive, you are retrieving a piece of your God-given power—the power with which you came. You are raising your vibrations as well as liberating your *Self* and others from a prison of inertia. By making the conscious decision to accomplish wellness within your *Self*, you automatically open the door to being able to forgive.

I often ask the question, "Are you individual or separate?" Think about it. . . .

Yes. We are individual, but the adversarial influences would have us feel separate, because if we view ourselves as separate we tend to feel "picked on" and alone. We don't feel a part of the whole. We may even feel everyone is against us or see ourselves as victims. When we experience these kinds of feelings we have little sense of belonging. On the other hand, when we feel we belong, we don't view others as our enemies. We are more apt to feel a sense of connectedness or togetherness, of unity. We desire sharing our good and Be-ing contributive.

Forgiving old hurts and new hurts is essential in achieving connectedness. Letting go of hurts from the past allows you to release others from captivity, and—more importantly—to release your *Self* at the same time.

If your parents are the target of your resentment, it's helpful to remember that they probably did the best they could or knew how under the circumstances. Who knows what role models they had as children. Your parents may not have had their emotional needs met. Perhaps they were victims. Undoubtedly they were hurt and had no idea how to resolve that hurt. Historically, parents of that generation didn't talk much about their feelings. As children they were not allowed to express how they felt or what they thought. They had very little understanding of the psychology of human behavior.

Who sets out to harm their children on purpose? Do any of us really intend to hurt them and leave emotional scars? Is it possible that many parents came from a lack of emotional stability in some area of their lives?

If you are having a difficult time forgiving a parent, I invite you to close your eyes and see if you can visualize them as a child . . . Look for them until you find them as that child. Upon finding them, go into their heart. Sense their hurt, their vulnerability, their confusion, their sense of rejection or of being alone. Where did those feelings come from? Could you forgive the person who created a parent's pain when they were a child? Could you go back further and forgive the person who created that pain—and continue going back, forgiving until you come to where the original pain began? Yes—just where *did* that pain begin?

Forgiving may be the most difficult thing you ever do. By not forgiving, however, according to Holy Writ, "There remaineth in you the greater sin." In other words, one's refusal to forgive a sinner (someone who missed the mark) is considered a worse sin than the sin to be forgiven. For those of you who are Christian, the criterion of all criterion—are some of the last words Christ spoke as he hung on the cross: "Father, forgive them, for they know not what they do" (Luke 23:34). Can't we forgive someone who did much less to us than was done to the Savior?

If it is difficult forgiving your enemies, it is even more difficult forgiving your loved ones. You care about them and often have to go on living or struggling with them.

Because of this, there is the possibility that they can continue hurting you.

Yes, our families are often the greatest source of our trials. By holding onto resentment, anger, hurt, or other negative feelings towards a family member, however, we separate our *Self* from them. In doing this, we give up a piece of our *Self*. We dis-connect a part of our identity that is essential for our growth. Consequently, moving forward as a whole person becomes very difficult when that part of us is missing. Our *Self* worth and feelings of belonging are undermined, since humans require a sense of connectedness to feel complete.

When feeling separate and dis-connected from family members, your heart is incessantly heavy. If you avoid forgiving, you may experience a feeling of alienation or helplessness. No matter what the unresolved feeling is between you and a loved one, there can be no resolution without forgiveness—without *your* forgiveness. Let all conditions and expectations go! Quit counting and tear up the score sheet! Don't wait for the other person to extend an apology or offer forgiveness. If you expect them to do so, you might consider some self-evaluation to determine whether your ego is still in the way.

I had a singular experience with my deceased father a few years ago that indelibly placed in my mind the eternal ramifications of un-forgiveness. I will give you some background before I share my experience.

My dad was a gentle and quiet man. He was also selfless and kind. As soft-spoken as he was, I didn't like to be in his presence if he ever got angry. He held things in until something would finally trigger him, like the straw that breaks the camel's back, and then he would erupt. But even these eruptions were mild and short lived. Nevertheless, I didn't like seeing this side of him because he wasn't the person I knew during the episodes. Even as a youth, I realized he had some hidden anger, as anyone might had they experienced a childhood like his.

My father was an only child. When he was eleven his parents died in the flu epidemic of 1918 three days apart. He was then left to be raised by his maternal grandparents. Dad's life from that point on must have been extremely difficult, as he would never talk about it. My mother occasionally gave me and my brothers a glimpse of what he had endured. Evidently Dad did all the housecleaning, the laundry (by hand), and the meals for himself and his grandparents. Because of his grandmother's physical condition, attitude and strictness he was disallowed friends in the house, nor was he allowed to go to parties. It was as if she didn't want him to have any fun, I came to understand upon interviewing him about his life. At age 15 it was necessary for Dad to quit school and go to work to help support his grandparents. When he got older, if he went out with his friends he always had to be home by nine o'clock. Putting it mildly, he had a lonely, difficult and very unhappy childhood.

Dad had a brilliant mind. His thirst for knowledge was unquenchable, and he evidently felt cheated at having to quit school to meet his grandmother's demands. One of his earliest jobs was cleaning the yards around an office building where he later became office manager. This was a large lumber company in Arizona. Because of the large number of Mexicans employed by this company, Dad learned to speak Spanish fluently. Somewhere along the way, he was finally able to go to night school and become an accountant. My father was a very hard worker and loyal employee. Starting from the bottom and working up, he eventually became the Comptroller of this same company, one of the largest corporations in Arizona. He was greatly valued and appreciated by his employers. He worked for this company for 64 years and also developed several businesses of his own. Dad passed away in 1985, shortly before his 78th birthday.

The following experience took place about two years after his passing.

One day I was lying on a bed with my eyes closed, processing some very deep feelings. Suddenly there was my father—in my Spiritual mind—extremely anguished, pacing back and forth. Crying and shaking his head, he kept saying "I can't progress, I can't progress." All he could do was pace back and forth and say, "I can't progress, I can't progress!" He didn't look at me, but seemed to know I was watching. "Dad, what's the matter? What's wrong?" I said. He continued to pace, still crying and exclaiming, "I can't progress, I can't progress." He was extremely distraught! He wouldn't stop and tell me what the problem was, so I started looking around to see if I could find some way to understand his plight.

The next moment I saw his grandmother standing at a distance. She was very sorrowful, with her head bowed. She also seemed to be crying. Instantly I knew what this scene was all about. My father had not forgiven his grandmother! I turned back to him. "Dad, you've got to forgive her!" (He knew who I was talking about.) He responded, "I can't. I can't," and kept pacing. "Dad, you have to forgive her." Once again he answered, "I can't, I can't," at which point I began reasoning with him: "Dad, she did the best she knew how. She was probably in deep despair and anger over losing your mother in the prime of life. Perhaps you were a constant reminder of her loss, and she resented you being the one who was left. Dad, she didn't hurt you on purpose. She was just suffering from her own grief and anguish. She didn't know how to deal with her feelings, so she took it out on you. She probably didn't realize how miserable she made your life. Look at her, Dad. She is very sorry for what she has done. But *you* have to forgive her so these many years of anger, resentment, and strife can be healed.

At some level I understood that Dad's grandmother had also been unable to move forward because of his un-forgiveness. This un-forgiveness had literally held them both captive.

As I continued to reason with Dad, all of a sudden he was with his grandmother. They were embracing and crying profusely on one another's shoulders. The much needed healing was finally taking place after many years! (She died when Dad was 25.) As I was rejoicing in my heart for what was transpiring, I saw Dad's mother standing beside them with tears in her eyes, hugging both of them. She seemed very grateful and relieved this hour had finally come! Then I saw Dad's grandfather standing in the distance with a pleased expression, as if to say, "At long last, this healing is finally taking place."

From this experience, I came to a much deeper understanding of the true significance and supreme importance of forgiving. Appreciation for the healing and freeing power of this beautiful principle increased within me a million-fold!

If you don't feel ready to forgive yet, ask yourself how holding onto old hurt, resentment, bitterness, and pain is serving you? Do you need it? Which would you rather have, pain and no gain, or peace and progression?" Listen to your thoughts while asking these questions because your thoughts are expressing your *Self*.

When your thirst for inner peace is acute enough, you will find the internal commitment to do whatever is necessary to gain that peace. You will strive diligently to eliminate your less than glorious feelings, thoughts, attitudes, and behaviors. You will extend total forgiveness to those whom you feel have wronged you.

It may help to remember that forgiveness does not mean you condone what someone did. They remain accountable for their deeds, as do we all. Therefore, forgiving does not mean that we are saying what they did was okay. This misconception is often the stumbling block to forgiving for most of us, and particularly those who have suffered abuse.

Perhaps they think if they forgive they are accepting the perpetrator's behavior or saying the violation was acceptable. Because they cannot bring themselves to excuse the behavior in question—understandably—they feel they cannot forgive. In such cases it helps to remember that forgiving does *not* mean condoning, or excusing the behavior.

It does mean that instead of harboring the old negative energy created by the incident, they are finally transforming that energy—letting go of the enmity and anger in their heart. It can no longer choke their life! They are no longer stuck! They can progress!

Remind your *Self* that holding on to un-forgiveness is not worth staying parked in the rut that prevents you from going forward on your journey.

While you are in the process of forgiving others, it is also extremely important that you forgive yourself. Often we continue blaming ourselves for something not of our making, especially if we have been abused and made to feel it was our fault. Therefore, we hold onto the guilt created by abuse and believe we are a *bad* person and there is no way to overcome being bad. Do your best to acknowledge the reality of the situation that has made it difficult for you to forgive yourself. Be willing to love your *Self* enough to forgive "you."

A friend shared something she found helpful in visualizing the "letting go" aspect of forgiveness. She would picture whoever she needed to forgive floating away from her. She saw them holding in their hands whatever deed or violation they had committed that she wished to forgive. She realized that although the person who hurt her would have to live with their deed, she could choose not to—she could let the violation go. It was no longer her problem. She found it also helped to imagine the person floating far enough away that they could no longer reach her with the deeds they held.

Whenever she visualized this, all the anger, resentment, and bitterness toward the person floated away also. These were good things to lose. She pictured them being absorbed in the infinite Love of the Universe and she felt light and clear, ready to get on with life. She noticed that in most cases, a feeling of compassion for the offender would arise, though they were not present and possessed no awareness of the change in her feelings. It was as if there was now room for compassion because the blocked space had been cleared by the anger and hurt floating away.

Re-claim your intrinsic power. Forgive! Forgiving is what you do for yourself in your quest to become whole. And what is the wonderful by-product of forgiveness? Those whom you forgive also benefit! You have better things to do with your life than to dwell on the negativity of the past and allow it to have power over you.

If you get *stuck* in forgiving someone, realize it does not all have to be accomplished at once. Take it in stages, if that helps. Remember, forgiving is something you do for yourself—you're the one in charge. Utilize whichever tool you find works most effectively in accomplishing forgiveness. Do your best to reach all the layers, levels, areas, and aspects of you that still need healing.

If you continue to struggle with forgiving someone, another stumbling block that may be in your path is *pride*. Perhaps your ego has something vested in holding on to un-forgiveness. Once again, go inside and ask yourself what you can gain by this. When you eliminate pride you ultimately experience a liberation that only comes with the dismissal of your jailer—your inner enemy.

Thus far, we have been discussing the moral aspect of forgiving. If we could only see what un-forgiveness does to our energy field—how it affects us physically and internally. If we could see what it does to our body chemistry, to each cell, to every inch and fiber of our Be-ing—we would certainly be motivated into action. For instance, have you ever heard of cancer, of gall stones, heart problems, liver problems, and such? I think you get the picture.

Just understanding the health consequences of *un-forgive-ness* is reason enough to forgive.

All sickness and unhappiness comes from violating the Laws of Love, and not forgiving is at the top of the list. By healing un-forgiveness, much sickness and unhappiness can be eliminated.

Most of all, consider what un-forgiveness does to your Spirit, to your Soul. When you refuse to forgive, the *spark* of your Spirit—the very essence of your *Be-ing*—is damaged. Your vibrations are lowered, which makes you vulnerable to more powerful negative influences. Little by little you become hardened and further distance yourself from God, leaving you to wonder what has happened to "you."

Forgiveness of *Self* is imperative. We usually have a difficult time forgiving ourselves because of feeling unworthy, imperfect, not enough, or not good enough (there is a difference). Consider forgiving your *Self* first for not being perfect, worthy, enough or good enough. Then forgive your *Self* for any shame and guilt you might feel for something you did or didn't do; for the things you feel you've done wrong or are holding against your *Self.* (These feelings about our *Self* are some of humankind's greatest blocks.) If you are unable to forgive your *Self*, it's almost impossible to genuinely forgive another. Why is forgiving your *Self* a good place to start?

As children we often mistakenly believe we are the cause of any abuse inflicted upon us. We may have been made by the perpetrator to feel that we brought it on ourselves and, therefore, deserved the abuse. Forgiving ourselves is a way to clear the unfounded guilt our Child may be carrying.

Our Child aspect desperately needs validation that any abuse suffered was not his/her fault.

In addition to forgiving others and ourselves, it is cleansing to ask others to forgive offenses for which we are responsible. Asking forgiveness goes hand in hand with extending forgiveness. In other words, when we receive pardon from others, it pardons the same in them.

Isn't this what is meant in the Lord's Prayer when it says, "And forgive us our debts, as we forgive our debtors. Forgive us our trespasses as we forgive our trespassers"? If we think it's possible to hurt another person or another living thing without hurting ourselves, we are mistaken. By extending to others our total forgiveness, we create an energy shift that enables us to receive the same in return.

As you forgive, you prepare your *Self* to return from the detour you took on your journey. Stumbling blocks simply dissipate. And because forgiveness is one of the greatest solvents on earth, the wall which has held you prisoner begins to crumble and allows your freedom. Neville tells us that "Freedom and forgiveness are indissolubly linked. Not to forgive is to be at war with ourselves, for we are freed according to our capacity to forgive."

You may be surprised how your life opens up for you as you forgive. You will also experience a sense of relief and freedom you have never felt before. Returning to the main road is a magnificent feeling!

CHAPTER 16

Accomplishing Forgiveness

Anger makes you smaller,
while forgiveness forces you to grow beyond what you were.
—Cherie Carter-Scott

So . . . where do you start with the forgiveness process? If you are asking this question, might I suggest you begin by Scripting for the ability to forgive yourself.

The following are three areas of common weaknesses that keep a person from moving forward in the forgiving process. They are:

Inability to forgive Self

No desire to forgive those who need forgiveness

Resistance and unwillingness to face own issues

There are also helpful suggestions to get you started. They are examples of what I would say if I were doing it for my *Self.* However, feel free to tailor the Scripting to your needs.

1) Script: "Spirit, please locate the origin of the feelings that cause my inability to forgive myself." Or, "please

locate the origin of the feelings which keep me from forgiving myself." Continue through the rest of the Script and at the replacement (the second blank line), perhaps you would say, "**I choose** forgiving myself for anything I view as unforgivable." (Name it if you have something specific in mind). "**I feel** forgiveness of myself for (whatever). **I am** forgiving myself for (whatever). I allow myself the mistakes from which I have learned, and let it be all right. I don't need to be perfect right now. I give myself permission to learn and grow in wisdom and truth. **I choose** improving each day. **I feel** myself improving daily. **I am** improving day by day. **I choose** peace, **I feel** peaceful, **I am** peaceful."

(Note: It is important to state, "**I choose, I feel, I am**" with each Scripting. The *feeling* of the attribute is the missing link and creates the bridge between the *choosing* of it and the *Be-ing* of it.

2) Script: "Spirit, please locate the origin of my feelings of resistance to forgiving those whom I need to forgive. Locate the origin of my feelings that keep me from having the desire to forgive others." Continue through the Script, and at the replacement (the second blank line) perhaps you could say, "I choose forgiving each and every person for whom I have felt anger, resentment, disdain, hostility, hate, or, unforgiveness. These feelings are keeping me in bondage. I give myself permission to forgive all whom I need to forgive. I feel forgiving of everyone. I am forgiving of all."

This doesn't mean your work is complete. The Script is

opening the door and allowing you to look at each person for whom you have held malice in your heart. When the time is perfect, you will know each person who requires your forgiveness. An opportunity will arise allowing you that experience.

    3) Script: "Spirit, please locate the origin of my feelings of resistance and unwillingness to look at my own issues. Locate the origin of the feelings keeping me from the desire to see my own issues or weaknesses."

Continue through the rest of the Script, and at the replacement (the second blank line) perhaps you could say,

"I choose supporting myself in growing emotionally and spiritually. I feel this support from my *Self.* I am supportive of my *Self* in taking responsibility for my own issues and weaknesses. I choose being focused in resolving and healing old issues. I feel focused while doing so. I am focused on resolving my feelings. I give my *Self* permission to resolve and heal my less than glorious characteristics. I feel like healing. I am happy in my quest to resolve and heal old, unnecessary issues that do not serve me for good."

By processing these three areas of probable weakness, you may better prepare for the errand that lies before you. Any time you feel resentments, anger, hurts, or wounds resonating inside, quickly Script for those feelings. When you make the commitment to alleviate old mind-sets, your Spirit, True *Self,* Higher *Self* offers plenty of opportunities to get in touch with the feelings, people, places, circumstances, and events that require forgiveness. Be aware that every aggravating occurrence which comes into your life from this point forward is mirroring to you what needs to be resolved. Be grateful for this "gift." Sometimes you won't particularly like the package the gift comes wrapped in, but acknowledge it as a gift and find the lesson you need to learn therein. Continue resolving feelings elicited from these experiences until you find the peace you desire.

How long do you process forgiving? For those of you who are Christian, how many times did Christ suggest that we forgive? Wasn't it 70 times seven? And how many is that? 490 times! Could He possibly have meant that we are to forgive one person 490 times?

Many years ago, before the Script was introduced to me, my husband and I took a class from a beautiful woman who taught us the importance of forgiveness. She suggested we literally forgive one person 490 times if we truly desired to experience the healing, the releasing and the liberating effects this kind of forgiveness brings. The big question was, how do we go about forgiving 490 times?

Because numerous people have utilized this process and received amazing results, I am pleased to share it with you. If you choose participating, you can also experience how cleansing and freeing this kind of forgiving is, and the inner healing that results from it.

Our instructor suggested that our earthly father, bearing the seed of our creation, is the person with whom we begin. So . . . locate a big notepad and a pen or pencil. Sit down and write "I," (then your name) "forgive my father (or Dad) for _____(write in whatever you desire to forgive)." Then complete the statement by writing, "and release him to his highest good." As you know, we keep people from moving on to their highest good by holding on to our un-forgiveness.

Here is an example: "I, Karol, forgive my father for humiliating me in front of my friends when I was ten years old, and I release him to his highest good." That's it. But that's only once. Recall, if you will, that all feelings, thoughts, memories, words, people, places, circumstances, and events have a positive or negative energy charge. Every experience leaves something with you. If the energy connected with what you are forgiving makes a shift and dissipates after writing the statement the first time, you then go on to the next one. But, if you don't feel the incident has really been forgiven—if there has not been an energy shift—then write it out again. Write it out as many times as necessary to neutralize any charge remaining inside you.

When you no longer feel an energy charge involved with the incident, person, or feeling, it's time to process another incident or feeling. In reality, you may write about one issue two times, ten times, or even 60 times. Pay close attention to how you feel *inside* each time you write a "Forgiveness." Continue writing until the energy of that one feeling or incident is totally changed, shifted, discharged, or transformed—until you no longer feel a need to write another forgiveness for that issue.

This story illustrates the effectiveness of writing out "Forgivenesses." I worked with a 52-year-old man whose parents were a very strict German couple. He was the older of two boys, and farming was their vocation. He said that as a boy and young man he could never do anything right, and his younger brother could never do anything wrong (according to his father). I could see the hurt in him from what I learned were years of yearning for acceptance from his father. The hurt stuck at a deep level. Nevertheless, he was a brave and loving son.

I shared this process with John while visiting him and his wife. One morning he joined me in the living room and I could tell he had been crying. There was a far-away look in his eyes as he sat down. Then he looked at me and said, "I cannot believe what just happened to me."

He explained that he started writing his Forgivenesses, and as he wrote "I, John, forgive my father for never accepting me for who I am," he started crying like a child. He cried and cried for two pages, writing the same thing over and over again. He wrote the Forgivenesses more than 100 times before the unresolved feeling finally dissipated and he was truly able to experience forgiveness toward his father. Such an overwhelming peace came over John that he had difficulty comprehending it. The wound in his heart was finally healing! Later he continued to write, eventually completing the 490 times. His whole demeanor was transformed upon completing this activity.

Sometimes a person needs to write one Forgiveness many times before the feeling is healed. If this is the case, after 100 times as with John, you have only 390 more Forgivenesses to write out. They can be on any other issue, or on as many issues as is necessary.

Even if you feel you have nothing to forgive, you might be surprised once you get started. No matter how good a parent is, how much they love you, or how much you love them, seldom does any child get through life without being adversely affected in some way growing up. These incidents may seem very insignificant when they occur. Nevertheless, they can still impact the emotional *Self*; unknowingly they are held somewhere inside until they are resolved.

We also hold feeling energies from experiences with our siblings. Although there may be happy memories of our childhood, it would be highly unusual not to have unre-solved negativity registering somewhere inside. We might think we have dismissed challenges we had with brothers or sisters, but in truth, a re-solution is still in order—usually something needs to be fixed. Perhaps there have been too many mis-communications, assumptions, expectations, inconsistencies, besides the inability to express how we felt or feel. We may have learned to tolerate them, but these conditions take their toll on relationships. Until the neces-sary resolution takes place, we are not free to be our True *Self*.

Your family is your greatest institution of learning, so be grateful for them, regardless of what needs fixing. Where else can you go to learn more about relationships, about forgiveness, or acceptance and love? If you ever needed to change your perceptions—the ones that began in your early years—the family might be a good place to start.

Within the family unit we have the opportunity to exer-cise forgiveness, to feel love, learn compassion, extend respect, and establish unity. We have the opportunity to develop a benevolent attitude. If we are unable to experi-ence these qualities within the family unit, how can we expect to embrace our neighbor, our community, and our fellowman, "out there?"

Find it within your heart to heal old mis-understandings with any of your siblings. If you have a tendency to see everything that is "wrong" with them, look inside. What are they mirroring to you about yourself? Are they an inner enemy? The same thing applies to your parents. What do you need to forgive where they are concerned?

Some people might say, Well, there's nothing to forgive my father (my mother, or siblings). That was the case with me. But I knew it was important to do this forgiving process for each suggested person (Dad, Mom, and others not yet mentioned) in case I did have something on a subconscious level that needed resolving. So, I sat with the intent of healing anything I needed to heal with my father, letting my right brain (intuitive) roam. Unless you are very much aware of what you need to forgive, it is best not to dwell in your left brain (logical). Don't try to "figure it out." Relax and let go of expectations on any level.

To integrate the functions of both sides of my brain, I closed my eyes and took a very deep breath through my nose and let it out slowly through my mouth. I took another deep breath and at the top of the breath, I held it three counts before exhaling slowly through my mouth again. In a few minutes, feelings and incidents began surfacing. There weren't many, but the ones that came to mind were important to resolve. I kept going for as long as the thoughts, feelings, and memories came.

Depending upon how much time you are willing to spend, the process of writing out Forgivenesses can take days or even weeks to accomplish. Don't be in a hurry. You are dealing with years of accumulated energies. Let the feelings and thoughts just flow.

Incidents will even come to you while you go about your daily routine. If you are unable to stop and write when this happens, make a note of your thought so you can write out the Forgiveness at a later time. For the best results, continue this process until the 490 Forgivenesses for your father are completed.

The next person for whom you write Forgivenesses is your mother. Follow the same procedure as with your father. "I, Karol, forgive my mother for _____-_____, and release her to her highest good."

Why do we do this process with our father and mother first? Before conception, at conception, and during gestation we were greatly influenced by our parents. From them we inherited feelings, thoughts, attitudes and beliefs through our genetic coding. According to the woman from whom we learned this process, we forgive Dad first because he was the seed that made it possible for us to have life; and Mom because she carried and gave us birth. Some people have a difficult time with this order, feeling that Mom had the greater role through the nine months, giving birth and caring for us as children. All I can say is . . . this is the way I learned it. Do it however you choose. It will work either way. Simply experience it.

Are you wondering who the third person is that you forgive? Well, this is interesting. You forgive either the doctor, the mid-wife or the cab driver—whoever touched or handled you first as they brought you into this sphere of existence.

When I was writing Forgivenesses for the doctor, I felt moved to include the hospital personnel, at which point some very deep feelings began surfacing. (Those of you who have read *Feelings Buried Alive Never Die . . .* may remember the account of my birth and understand one of the reasons it was so charged with energy.) Also, I later discovered that I had felt violated by one of the nurses tending to me. Evidently she treated me with extreme roughness—as if she were very angry at someone and took it out on me. I was really amazed how my subconscious started spilling out feelings of which I had no conscious memory or awareness. In talking with others who have participated in this process, I found that each of them has been amazed and deeply affected.

When you complete forgiving the doctor or any hospital personnel (which will probably not take 490 times unless you experienced trauma or a long stay in the hospital), you may have a desire to further forgive your *Self* using this same process. After forgiving these four people, you may choose who will be next if you feel inspired to continue— perhaps a brother or sister. You will know if you need to. Quite often, however, upon forgiving Dad, Mom, doctor and *Self*—nothing else really bothers you anymore about anyone. Or what previously bothered you suddenly becomes very insignificant.

The results of using this process are truly remarkable! Perhaps it's one more of those gifts that life serves up on a silver platter when we are willing to accept responsibility, be accountable, and incorporate true healing principles into our life.

If you still feel there is unresolved business with someone, be diligent in processing those feelings in the same manner. Use this forgiveness process if, for instance, you have an abusive spouse or employer. From time to time you may need to get out your pad and pencil to write more Forgivenesses for a person you have already completed the

490 times. If you interact with that person only on occasion, feelings of which you hadn't been aware may still come to the surface.

This happened to me with my mother a few years after I had written the 490 Forgivenesses for her. She and my step-father came to stay with us for about ten days, after which my husband and I drove them to California to visit my brother. The night we arrived there, I found it necessary to sit down and write some forgivenesses for her before I could go to sleep. Their ten-day stay and the seven hour trip brought up issues and feelings I thought were resolved. After writing the Forgivenesses, I was fine. I had to remind myself that what I was feeling was *my* problem—not hers.

The important lesson I learned from this process is that we can achieve a very significant resolution when we have a sincere desire and the tools to heal old hurts, wounds, and pain. God is pleased with our intent to do this, and He honors our endeavors. He even sends heavenly helpers when we request them, particularly while doing the forgiveness process.

For several years after completing my Forgivenesses I didn't have occasion to suggest this process and had forgotten about it. In the Spring of 1992 I received a phone call from Sue, who was feeling total despair. She was on the verge of ending her own life when she first made an appointment with me a few months earlier. She was having major difficulty in working through her challenges. While talking with her this time, I was somewhat at a loss for a course of action. We had already done so much processing. I found myself thinking, where do I go from here? and said a little prayer. As I continued to talk with Sue, suddenly I remembered the forgiveness process and explained it to her. She agreed to give it a try and began that night.

The next day, Sue telephoned again. I could tell by the sound of her voice that she had already accomplished a major energy shift. Her voice sounded totally different! Peace and tranquillity had replaced hopelessness and anxiety. "Oh, Karol, I've only written 130 Forgivenesses, but I cannot believe how different I feel!" And then she added, "But I have to confess that I started with my mother first because I knew my main issues were with her." I encouraged her to do whatever worked for her.

We talked about the process, and Sue bubbled with excitement! She loved writing these Forgivenesses and the subsequent feelings that resulted. Her enthusiasm for completing the procedure was unbounded! After saying goodbye, she continued doing it the way she had started.

Sue called back about 30 hours later. "Karol, you're never going to believe this. As I was sitting here writing these Forgivenesses for my mother, I began to feel so terrible inside. I was remembering all the things I needed to forgive and saying awful things about her. I thought how disappointed she would be if she knew what I was doing. (Her mother had passed away the previous year.) Then all of a sudden, I knew my mother was standing right there—next to me—helping me. And she could hardly wait for me to finish!"

Sue is quite intuitive, visual, and sensitive, so I didn't doubt that she could sense her mother's spirit standing next to her, encouraging her to complete these Forgivenesses. "I finally had to go to bed at 2:30," she said, "because I was getting sick. But when I awoke in the morning, I knew my mom was sitting at the foot of my bed, waiting for me to get up and finish. So, I finished, and I feel like I've been let out of prison!" Sue's exhilaration was something to behold!

Sue so thoroughly enjoyed basking in the light of her newly found freedom that she waited a while before processing Forgivenesses for her father. Recognizing the depth of healing that took place with her mother, she delighted in repeating the process with her father. From doing this, a transformation took place in every facet of Sue's Be-ing! I had never seen nor felt such remarkable change in a person in so short a time. It was phenomenal! And the difference it made continues serving her daily. Other issues still needed processing over the course of time, but her very deep-seated issues had been resolved through writing Forgivenesses.

This process literally works miracles with people's feelings and with the attitudes of entire families. Darla, a 43-year-old woman, had been at odds with her mother practically all her life. She grew up on a Midwest farm in a family of eight children. For some reason she never felt a closeness to her mother. In fact, as Darla expressed it, her mother wouldn't even give her the time of day. Consequently, Darla was not prepared for what happened after she wrote Forgivenesses for her mom.

Darla lived in Las Vegas, Nevada at this time, and though her mother knew nothing about Darla doing this process, it was as if her mom did an about face. From that point on, Darla's mother couldn't do enough for Darla! Remember, not a word was said about this to her mother. Mom just felt an unconscious change in energy and responded to it. Darla and her mother had finally become friends. They continue to be good friends, enjoying each other's company more than ever before. Yes, the energy shift between two people is miraculous when this process is used!

Another example: Greg was the eldest of six children and had been raised on a ranch in the Southwest. He had three younger sisters and when he was 12 years old, a brother was finally born. At an early age, Greg was given many heavy responsibilities by his father, who was very particular. No matter how hard Greg tried to do things right as he carried out his assigned duties, he could never do them good enough for his father. Something was always wrong. Greg was never commended or encouraged. His internal programming eventually became one of, "I can never do anything right."

With Greg's perception that he always displeased his father, he grew up feeling dad was untouchable, literally. Therefore, Greg could never put his arm around dad. Even in his late forties, Greg still felt the need to please this parent. Greg learned about the forgiveness process. As he diligently wrote his 490 Forgivenesses, he was surprised at the memories that surfaced. A lot of deep hurts had been buried over the years. Greg dealt with them one by one as he wrote out the Forgivenesses. When he finally finished, he was greatly relieved.

Greg and his father lived in different communities, so it was some time after Greg completed this process before he saw his father. Upon greeting each other, and without conscious thought, Greg not only touched his father without recoiling, but put his arm around him, expressing love without any effort or holding back. To Greg, this was a major break-through in their relationship. The old feelings never returned, and Greg was truly able to appreciate his father's good points for the first time in his life.

Many of us have a love/hate relationship with one or both parents (or other family members). By writing out what needs to be forgiven in our relationships we initiate beautiful healing. A love/love relationship with our parents is much more rewarding and fulfilling than a love/hate relationship. On occasion, an old, hurtful feeling may rear its ugly head. If this happens, simply Script or write out another forgiveness for that particular feeling until the energy charge dissipates.

Remember, there are years of accumulated, buried feelings in each of us. We may require several months to work through energy-charged feelings, especially if our parents are still living and we interact with them on a daily basis.

If undesirable feelings come between us and our parents (or other family members), remember, they are only mirroring to us the feelings *we* need to resolve. Instead of our associations being uncomfortable, they can be wonderful opportunities to heal old feelings we have not yet addressed.

While writing our initial Forgivenesses, we may inadvertently omit some issues. Keep in mind, forgiving is a process—we are on a journey. We are chipping away at our worn out, less than glorious feelings. We are bringing down our wall and preparing ourselves to open the door that reconnects us with the Love that we are—with our heart of gold.

Here is another example of the power of releasing someone with forgiveness. There was a family of seven adult brothers and sisters whose father was in his late 80's.

Wayne, the father, had been a good, honest, upstanding man, but he was somewhat difficult to get along with and hard to please. His siblings had all lived long lives into their 90's, and there was every indication that Wayne would also. However, his health started to deteriorate and it appeared as if his time to go was imminent. But he hung on for months. It seemed that nothing was ever going to change.

One of Wayne's sons, Sam, had been through this forgiveness process. He knew that even though his brothers and sisters loved their father, there were buried, negative feelings that needed to be forgiven. Sam took it upon himself to suggest to the others that writing out Forgivenesses for their father might be a step in the right direction. Surprisingly, they all agreed to participate.

Sam wasn't one to ask his siblings if they had completed the process. He would wait and let them tell him if and when they finished. One of Sam's sisters was taking the responsibility for the primary care of both parents. Interestingly, she had some of the deepest issues with their father. She phoned Sam one day, and in a choked voice thanked him for suggesting the family write Forgivenesses for dad. She knew that had she not done these Forgivenesses, her attitude toward her father would have been unbearable. Having forgiven, she was able to attend to him with patience, love, and compassion.

Six weeks after the brothers and sisters completed their lists of Forgivenesses, Wayne passed away. When he died, these siblings felt a unity and love that was exceptional and very beautiful to behold. Everyone in the family felt this unity and love, as did those in attendance at the viewing and the funeral.

Perhaps the greatest illustration of the power of forgiveness is found in George Ritchie's book, *Return From Tomorrow*. If you have read it, it bears repeating. If you haven't, you may be touched by its message.

When the war in Europe ended in May, 1945, the 123rd Evac entered Germany with the occupying troops. I was part of a group assigned to a concentration camp near Wuppertal, charged with getting medical help to the newly liberated prisoners, many of them Jews from Holland, France, and eastern Europe. This was the most shattering experience I had yet had; I had been exposed many times by then to sudden death and injury, but to see the effect of slow starvation, to walk through those barracks where thousands of men had died a little bit at a time over a period of years, was a new kind of horror. For many it was an irreversible process: we lost scores each day in spite of all the medicine and food we could rush to them.

And that's how I came to know Wild Bill Cody. That wasn't his real name. His real name was seven unpronounceable syllables in Polish, but he had long drooping handlebar mustaches like pictures of the old western hero, so the American soldiers called him Wild Bill. He was one of the inmates of the concentration camp, but obviously he hadn't been there long: his posture was erect, his eyes bright, his energy indefatigable. Since he was fluent in English, French, German and Russian, as well as Polish, he became a kind of unofficial camp translator.

We came to him with all sorts of problems; the paper work alone was staggering in attempting to relocate people whose families, even whole hometowns, might have disappeared. But though Wild Bill worked fifteen and sixteen hours a day, he showed no signs of weariness. While the rest of us were drooping with fatigue, he seemed to gain strength. "We have time for this old fellow," he'd say. "He's been waiting to see us all day." His compassion for his fellow-prisoners glowed on his face, and it was to this glow that I came when my own spirits were low.

So I was astonished to learn when Wild Bill's own papers came before us one day, that he had been in Wuppertal since 1939! For six years he had lived on the same starvation diet, slept in the same airless and disease-ridden barracks as everyone else, but without the least physical or mental deterioration.

Perhaps even more amazing, every group in the camp looked on him as a friend.

He was the one to whom quarrels between inmates were brought for arbitration. Only after I'd been at Wuppertal a number of weeks did I realize what a rarity this was in a compound where the different nationalities of prisoners hated each other almost as much as they did the Germans.

As for Germans, feeling against them ran so high that in some of the camps liberated earlier, former prisoners had seized guns, run into the nearest village and simply shot the first Germans they saw. Part of our instructions were to prevent this kind of thing and again Wild Bill was our greatest asset, reasoning with the different groups, counseling forgiveness.

"It's not easy for some of them to forgive," I commented to him one day as we sat over mugs of tea in the processing center. "So many of them have lost members of their families."

Wild Bill leaned back in the upright chair and sipped at his drink. "We lived in the Jewish section of Warsaw," he began slowly, the first words I had heard him speak about himself, "My wife, our two daughters, and our three little boys. When the Germans reached our street they lined everyone against a wall and opened up with machine guns. I begged to be allowed to die with my family, but because I spoke German they put me in a work group."

He paused, perhaps seeing again his wife and five children. "I had to decide right then," he continued, "whether to let myself hate the soldiers who had done this. It was an easy decision, really. I was a lawyer. In my practice I had seen too often what hate could do to people's minds and bodies. Hate had just killed the six people who mattered most to me in the world. I decided then that I would spend the rest of my life—whether it was a few days or many years—loving every person I came in contact with."

Loving every person—this was the power that had kept a man well in the face of every privation.

Notice that Wild Bill Cody lived on the same starvation diet and slept in the same airless and disease-ridden barracks as everyone else, but without the least physical or mental deterioration. How amazing! Wild Bill's attitude—the feeling in his heart and in his mind, because he had made it a conscious decision—was one of pure and simple love. He loved every person he came in contact with. In order to exhibit this depth of love, he would have *had* to forgive. What a sublime example of the profound and magnificent power of forgiveness and love!

I'm sure most of us have seen dreadful pictures of prisoners from the concentration camps and viewed historical accounts of the Holocaust. No matter the age, we have all been deeply affected by the Nazi atrocities that took place during World War II.

In the Spring of 1994, my 26-year-old son and I had the

opportunity to visit Dachau—one of these concentration camps. Over the years, I had seen hundreds of photographs and heard stories depicting this time in history, but none of them prepared me for the feelings that bombarded my heart while visiting Dachau: viewing graphic pictures of the conditions that existed in the prison camps; watching a historical film about how it all started; touring the facility and seeing the places of extermination. I had a very difficult time containing my feelings. Right now I can't find words for it. My eyes brim with tears just writing about it.

Even though I always found the story of Wild Bill Cody deeply touching, the magnitude of this man's spirit and his beautiful attitude became truly overwhelming for me after being at Dachau.

Could *we* do what Wild Bill did? His example behooves us to deal with each feeling and experience that needs resolution or forgiveness: abuse, neglect, abandonment, distrust, betrayal, rejection, anger, rage, Mom wasn't there for me. Dad always made me feel ignorant or guilty . . . whatever the case may be. Oh, that each of us could have the same fortitude and point of reference as Wild Bill Cody.

How about just cutting to the bottom line and forgiving it all? NOW! Like Wild bill did. Let your wall come tumbling down with no further resistance or hesitation!

It is called . . . *THE MIGHTY CHANGE.* Can you bring about this mighty change for the sake of the innate love, reverence, and respect you have for your True Self—your Divine Self? Strive to maintain the desire, courage, and commitment it takes for bringing this change into your life.

CHAPTER 17

Healing Old Relationships

All things are difficult before they are easy.

—Unknown

You now understand how Scripting and other processing tools can dismantle your wall, one block at a time. Yes, eventually it will be dismantled. However, you have just learned a faster way to remove the blocks without all the chiseling. You can simply dissolve the mortar and demolish the wall by choosing total forgiveness and unconditional love.

That is what Wild Bill did when he made the decision to forgive the soldiers who killed his family and to *love* every person with whom he came in contact. He applied the solvent that caused the blocks to come down very quickly. When faced with the split second decision he was called upon to make, he took a quantum leap!

Do you have any feelings that create negative energies and constrictions in your life? How much longer do you need them? Perhaps you can cut to the bottom line simply by deciding to love and forgive like Wild Bill did. However, if your mind set disallows letting go all at once, you may need to do some processing. You now have the tools of *Scripting, Vocalizing, Revising* and writing *Forgivenesses* for inappropriate feelings and thoughts. Doing any or all of these is powerful. Each tool is significant and has its place—especially if you like being independent of help from others. If this is the case, these processes will help you accomplish much on your own.

With these tools, and others you may know, there is something for assisting each of us to accomplish healing. Life is too short to let another day go by while we harbor unresolved feelings! Have the courage to open up the wound that needs to be examined. Realize that it will remain just that—an unhealed wound—until the core issue is addressed and re-solved. Whatever is un-resolved has caused a disconnection and contributed to inner conflict long enough. Be willing to initiate a re-connection with anyone from whom you may be estranged. Tell ego and pride to get out of your way!

Realize that through the years each of us has accumulated and buried countless unhealthy feelings—layers and layers deep. Consequently, varied appendages have spun off from them. These layers and their appendages may require consistent attention and processing to re-solve. Do your best to withdraw power from the feelings that have created unhealthy energies for so many years. You can be their master!

A few years ago I received a call from a woman who thanked me for *Feelings Buried Alive Never Die . . .* She was overjoyed! She and her daughters had been estranged for eight years. One of the daughters found the book and sent copies to her mom and sisters. This woman wanted to let me know that after they all read the book and Scripted their feelings, they were able to reconcile their differences and come together in love and understanding. She hadn't been this happy in years! Needless to say, it was truly gratifying to have her share this story.

How committed are we to eliminating residue from earlier hurts or assaults that have caused us suffering? How strong is our desire to heal each ache in our heart? How important is it to dismantle the wall that has been keeping us in prison? How deep is our desire to feel unconditional acceptance, forgiveness, love, peace, joy and compassion? Which is our destiny—to experience these qualities and live life to the fullest, or only experience a portion of it?

Are you willing to lead, without expectations, in healing a friendship or a relationship? (Remember, expectation is the basis of all disappointment.) Are you willing to come from your heart without needing to control the outcome? Can you come from love and understanding? As it says in the Prayer from St. Francis of Assisi, can you allow the other person to not understand you, but still do your best to understand them? Can you sincerely look, then see the situation through their eyes instead of your own? Can you allow what "is" and still love and accept the other person unconditionally—no matter what transpires?

This is what *Healing Feelings . . . From Your Heart* is all about—changing your inharmonious characteristics into harmonious ones; your weaknesses into strengths. Discover the Love that you are. Be the one who extends love, compassion, caring, and kindness to everyone, without expectations; be the peace maker through living your Truth.

Often, when we put forth the effort to discuss a misunderstanding with another, we find our words don't adequately express what we feel or would like to convey. Occasionally, although we ardently strive to make ourselves understood, we do more harm than good.

If you are in an undesirable situation with someone and feel the other person may not care to discuss it with you (or that talking to them wouldn't do any good), there is a beautiful process for achieving re-solution. But first, let me ask, "Are we fighting a *physical* battle or a *spiritual* battle in this life? Think about it . . . .

Because feelings are created in the subtle energy realm (spiritual realm) and they are something we cannot see, touch, smell, or hear, they do not create solid matter for us to view with our eyes. We *can* consciously direct these energies, but most of the time we don't.

Fundamental to our understanding is that in the subtle energy field there is no time or space. Consequently, it does not matter whether someone is in the next room or in the next state when you direct your feelings, thoughts, and dialogue to them. On some level they will receive the subtle energy of your message.

A powerful process evolved for me which has helped in healing some of the more challenging situations and interpersonal relationships I've encountered. I use this when someone mis-construes my intent and doesn't understand where I'm coming from, or when I feel that talking about it may be futile. If you are seeking a better outcome in similar situations, consider applying this silent process.

Find a quiet spot where you won't be disturbed. At night, just before you go to sleep, is an ideal time for doing this process. Both you and the other person are usually quiet and relaxed, allowing you to concentrate better and them to be more receptive to the process. Pray that God will help facilitate the desired outcome so healing can take place between you and the other person. Eliminate any need you might have to be *right* or to *win*. Script for any negativity you feel toward the person and replace it with the positive feelings you desire.

Take a few deep breaths, relax, and center yourself within. Go to your heart and feel all the love you're capable of feeling for the person with whom you are about to silently converse. See this person in your mind's eye. Send them love from your heart. Keep sending love. Do your best to see him or her the way God does. Let go of any negativity you feel toward the person, or any need you feel to "set them straight." Allow them to be who they really are.

It is extremely important that you come from love while doing this process, not blame or judgment—only love. Remove your defenses. When you have done these things, see the person in front of you in your mind's eye.

Now . . . mind to mind, heart to heart, or spirit to spirit (however you prefer designating it), begin talking to this person silently, letting your love flow while you speak. Tell them how much you appreciate them in your life and what you have learned from them. Enumerate their beautiful qualities—all that you admire about them. Be generous, but sincere. Let the person know how much you love them, or are striving to. Then ask, Spirit to Spirit, with all sincerity of heart (even if you feel you are not at fault), *"Will you forgive me for anything I may have mis-understood about your intent, or anything I have said or done that has hurt you?"* Then ask them to forgive you specifically, for the issue at hand.

Saying, I apologize or, Please forgive me, doesn't cut it. When you say, "Will you forgive me?" you are asking them a question. They are then included as part of the forgiveness process, which needs to go both ways. Give them time to assimilate all you are saying. Then say, "I behold you with eyes of love, and glory in your perfection." (Don't they deserve the best, which includes their perfection?) Then see your *Self* going up to this person, putting your arms around them and both of you embracing, left side to left side, literally heart to heart—*from* your heart. Hold them there as long as you like. Feel the energy change. When you are ready and sense you have accomplished your errand, leave them with love in your heart and gratitude for the healing that has been set in motion. Continue holding these positive feelings and pray for both of you each day.

Enjoy the feelings you experience during this process. Each time you finish conversing with someone Spirit to Spirit you can go to sleep with a smile on your face, knowing that healing is in progress.

Depending upon the severity of a conflict, doing the Spirit to Spirit process every night for several weeks will usually bring the desired results. The next time you see or talk with the one you've been processing, they will feel completely different toward you, but won't understand why. (The healing takes place in the subtle energy field first—the spiritual realm. Then it moves into the physical realm.) It's as if there was never a problem between you. Don't bring the issue up unless you feel strongly impressed to do so. Enjoy the forgiveness and love that has replaced the misunderstanding. Always extend your love silently as well as verbally.

When there is someone with whom you would like to resolve a misunderstanding, the most caring but disarming question you can ask is, "Karen (or whoever), will you forgive me?" If she doesn't answer you out loud, it's okay! Whether she responds verbally or not, Karen does respond. On some level, somewhere inside, she will respond, and usually the response comes from her heart—without even knowing.

Yes, subconsciously the person either accepts or rejects your request for forgiveness. Whichever it is doesn't matter. You have initiated your part of the responsibility. That's what is important. Be aware, however, of your motive in asking for forgiveness. If you are doing it simply to say you did—if the asking is done insincerely and not from the Love that you are—from your heart—the whole process will be ineffective. Recall that everyone is affected by what we do and say—good or not so good. By Be-ing sincere, you allow those around you to share the blessings of change along with you.

Several years ago, I learned something disturbing that a friend had said about me. I was totally surprised. I thought everything was fine between us. What was reported to me, in actuality, was far from true. My friend lived in a different city and we had not been in touch for nine months. Trying to clear up the misunderstanding over the phone would have been difficult, so I decided to talk to her Spirit to Spirit. After about ten days of doing this, my friend called our office to order some books. My husband talked with her. When she asked about me, he told her I would be in her city the following week. She asked him to have me call her and we would go to lunch.

We met at her home and she seemed sincerely happy to see me. There was no strain or indication that anything was wrong between us. During lunch she poured out her heart to me, sharing as she had always done. It was like old home week. We never spoke about what I had heard because it was not necessary. The negative energy was cleared between us and has remained that way.

I'm reminded of an experience one of my friends had with the Spirit to Spirit process. One day Kathy called me out of the blue. Our schedules were so busy we hadn't visited for over a year. She was catching me up on all that was going on in her life. Come to find out, she and her husband had been separated for awhile and he was planning to divorce her after 25 years of marriage. Naturally she was unhappy and wished she knew how to convince him to change his mind. There didn't seem to be any major reason for the divorce. As we talked I felt impressed to share the Spirit to Spirit process. She seemed somewhat interested and obtained the details of the procedure before we completed our conversation.

Two weeks later Kathy called again. "Karol, you'll never believe what has happened. You know that process you told me about two weeks ago? Well, I did it, and today Larry came by to tell me he had reconsidered the divorce. He wants us to get back together!"

Remind yourself constantly, while experiencing an interpersonal challenge, that all you need to do is clear out the negative energy that has been created. When the energy is changed, anything is possible. If you are the one having unhealthy feelings, you know what to do. If someone has directed negative energy your way, forgive and talk to them Spirit to Spirit. There's always a way to peaceably clear up the negative "vibes" that get in the way.

My desire is that your efforts give you the ability to experience freedom, and that you feel significant internal shifts as you move forward on your Feelings Journey. I have experienced the peace that is possible. I know the healing available for you if this is a route you choose. May your ultimate experience be one of light heartedness, boundless love, and absolute joy!

CHAPTER 18

A Grateful Heart

The depth of our gratitude
is commensurate with the depth of our understanding.

—Unknown

While Healing Feelings . . . From Your Heart, recall one of the most important fundamental truths in God's creation—the value of expressing **gratitude**. Being consciously aware of that for which we have to be grateful and articulating our gratitude daily is one of the most beautiful roads we can travel. And yet, for most of us, conveying our gratitude seems to be an afterthought rather than a primary characteristic.

Why are we slow to recognize the value of expressing gratitude—and then doing it? What if we cultivated the expression of gratitude as a daily practice in our lives? Gratitude to God, our family, neighbors, friends, and co-workers. Gratitude to everyone we come in contact with. So many people thirst desperately for an indication or mention of appreciation from family and acquaintances. Is it possible to do better by extending gratitude more consistently? How difficult can it be to compliment others for the good they do? Our expressed gratitude might make the difference in someone's entire day! (Incidentally, the ease with which a person expresses gratitude and appreciation is usually determined by how they feel about themselves.)

Each time you sincerely express gratitude to another— from your heart, with your heart—you are adding to the storehouse of your own blessings, of your own abundance. Begin expressing gratitude even if it's difficult at first. The more you do it, the easier it becomes. Your ultimate goal is to be able to actually *feel* gratitude with your heart as you express it. People know insincerity when they hear it; blessings only come when you are sincere.

If you have difficulty feeling gratitude, or are shy about expressing appreciation, perhaps there's a fear of what others are going to think, or of being spurned or rejected. These fears would be good to Script. Then step out of your fear and extend your *Self*. Take a chance. You will find that you receive more positive reactions than negative. And the positive will more than compensate for the negative.

Expressing gratitude softens the heart of the most miserable of souls. It brightens the darkest of days. The spirit of gratitude is continually pleasant and satisfying; from it emanates a sense of caring and helpfulness toward others. It generates love and friendship. It creates a congenial atmosphere.

Daily we are placed under obligation to one another— especially to friends and acquaintances. This sense of obligation generates feelings of thankfulness and appreciation— of gratitude—said to be the "memory" of the heart. It's natural for people to feel grateful to those who have done them a kindness, and the expression of gratitude is usually sufficient for the person who showed kindness.

Sometimes our sense of obligation and our gratitude is exploited. Often a favor is given with the deliberate intention of placing the recipient in a position of "owing" something back. Then gratitude becomes a debt that is expected to be paid. Remember—gratitude only means something when it is *freely* given. One is under no obligation to express it under manipulative circumstances. Gratitude cannot be owed.

Let us be truthful and honest when we extend a kindness, without any expectations of how we can benefit or gain. This is the most rewarding attitude.

You may remember when a man could stop on the highway and help someone change a flat tire or offer a ride without concern. As a young girl, I felt pleased when my father would help someone. This act of kindness was extended just for the satisfaction of helping. My dad never expected anything in return. What a sense of satisfaction this gave a person. How sad that in today's society it usually isn't safe to stop and offer this same assistance.

Edwin Arlington Robinson, distinguished American poet, once wrote:

> Two kinds of gratitude: the sudden kind we feel for what we take, the larger kind we feel for what we give.
>
> To most of us the first kind is the more familiar; that pleasure and warmth we feel when something is given to us. But we would agree, surely, that the second gratitude, while more rare, is more wonderful. How fine we feel when we have the opportunity to brighten the life of another; we feel deeply grateful for the opportunity to show our good will and our sense of Christian charity.

The gratitude we feel toward others is always more satisfying and rewarding than expecting others to express gratitude to us. By developing a grateful attitude we more readily see the boundless plenty in the world for which we can
be thankful. This helps the good outweigh the evil.

Gratitude initiates love and light. Love overpowers jealousy and other negative feelings, and light drives darkness
out of our lives. Conversely, feelings of pride and fear can
destroy our gratitude and establish selfishness. Through
conscious effort and a prayerful heart, we all have the capacity to cultivate a "gratitude attitude" toward God and
humankind! How much happier we all are in the presence
of a grateful and loving soul, including our own!

According to the apostle Paul, having an absence of
gratitude either to God or man, invites the presence of van-
ity and excessive self-sufficiency. As we travel through life,
often we get so caught up in our day to day challenges that
we assume a survival mode. In this mode, staying focused
on our noble intent is hard to do. It takes conscious effort
to enumerate, give thanks, or express gratitude for what we
are enjoying in life.

Extending gratitude is such a simple principle, and yet
we have to remind ourselves, and make a conscious effort to
remember to express it.

Have you ever known anyone who had a complaining
nature? How much of their time was spent dwelling on all
the things wrong with their life, rather than concentrating
on all that was *good* and on how much they were *blessed?*
When we look around and see the troubles and challenges
other people face daily, with whom would we trade places?

Gratitude

My thanks comes easily when my future rises and my
    will is king,
    and all the world seems my estate.
My thanks come easily such times, but wait—today let
    me reflect upon those thanks I own but which I find
    express themselves less fluently.
Today let me remember to give thanks not only for the
    sunlight
    but for those darker hours that teach me fortitude.
Let me profess today a grateful heart not merely for suc-
    cesses I may know,
    but as truly for those failures that teach humility.
Let me express my gratitude for all those petty inner
    conflicts which once resolved bring new serenity,
    and for those smaller distressing fears that have their
    ways of building such hope.
Let me breathe appreciation for all those poignant sights
    that teach me thoughtfulness, and wrongs that teach
    me fairness, and for each violated trust that leaves
    loyalty as its lesson.
And let me not forget today to whisper thanks for these:
The contempt that teaches pity,
The tear that teaches joy,
The pain that teaches mercy,
And the loneliness that teaches love.
So now let me reflect upon these things I own
    and let my thanks come easily today.

                              —Anonymous

Perhaps we would do well to express gratitude for all things. Even the undesirable things in our life, which ultimately take place for our growth, can be appreciated.

In the winter of 1989, after realizing how terribly amiss I was in this regard, I awoke one night and was unable to go back to sleep. I had company sleeping throughout my house, so I couldn't get up and do the things I usually do when I can't sleep. I lay awake wishing I could read, but without a book in my bedroom I began asking myself what else I could do to fill my time. My mind drifted to the desire I once had to someday write out gratitudes. I realized that this was the perfect opportunity for doing just that. But wait . . . I only had a pencil. I couldn't find any writing paper. So I began rummaging through the closet and dresser drawers. (My husband was out of town at the time, so I had no need to be quiet.) I finally found a huge ivory-colored Nordstrom's sack with brown diagonal lines running across it. Perfect! I took the sack and, between the lines, began writing out everything for which I was grateful. I had a wonderful time. I kept writing and writing and writing. It was so stimulating! In fact, thoughts came to me so rapidly that I couldn't write fast enough. After two hours, I finally ran out of things to be grateful for, but, I felt soooo good inside.

I concluded that those two hours were probably the best I'd spent in a long time. Before I drifted back to sleep, I decided to do my best to review what I had written every day. Due to the length of the list, I soon found it was taking too much time. Nevertheless, I desired having a daily reminder of that for which I was grateful, so I decided to record my gratitudes on tape, which I did. I made time to play them each morning while preparing for the day or working in the kitchen. Writing gratitudes gave me a singular sense of connectedness with Father in Heaven. I had never felt anything quite like it before. Talk about positive affirmations—these were the best!

If you would like a real high on a regular basis, just apply yourself to doing this little activity. If your experience is anything like mine, it will be one of the most uplifting, fulfilling, and satisfying endeavors you will ever participate in!

The World Is Mine

Today upon a bus, I saw a lovely maid
with golden hair;
I envied her—she seemed so gay—
and I wished I were as fair.
When suddenly she rose to leave,
I saw her hobble down the aisle;
She had one foot and wore a crutch,
but as she passed, a smile.

Oh, God, forgive me when I whine;
I have two feet—the world is mine!
And then I stopped to buy some sweets.
The lad who sold them had such charm.
I talked with him—he said to me:
"It's nice to talk with folks like you.
You see," he said, "I'm blind."
Oh, God, forgive me when I whine.
I have two eyes—the world is mine!

Then walking down the street,
I saw a child with eyes of blue,
He stood and watched the others play;
It seemed he knew not what to do.
I stopped for a moment, then I said,
"Why don't you join the others, dear?"
He looked ahead without a word.
And then I knew, he could not hear.
Oh, God, forgive me when I whine;
I have two ears—the world is mine!

With feet to take me where I'd go,
With eyes to see the sunset's glow,
With ears to hear what I would know,
Oh, God, forgive me when I whine;
I'm blessed, indeed! The World Is Mine!

—Unknown

GRATITUDE is the eternal law of increase, the complete power of Divine multiplication. The prayer of thanksgiving equals the law of plenty. Through sincere, heart-felt gratitude, the fullness of supply can be discharged in increasing abundance to more than fill the measure of one's needs.

CHAPTER 19

Revere Your "Self"

You were born an original. Don't die a copy.

—John Mason

You have heard how important it is to love others. You have heard that it's important to love your *Self*. But have you ever heard about "having reverence" for your *Self*?

Several years ago, after learning many new principles and gaining fresh understanding, I generally went through each day with my customary attitude. This attitude had to be monitored constantly so as not to be negative. Once in a while, however, my ego would take over.

Without realizing what I was doing, I would begin to exhibit characteristics of haughtiness, becoming puffed up from having gained new insights and knowledge. Then without seeing it coming, the "props" would be knocked out from under me! It was as if I had progressed to the twelfth grade only to fall back to the third—at which point I would have to begin the steps of improvement all over again. When I again reached the previous level, I would be fine for a while, then invariably repeat the same pattern.

Each time this regression took place it became more difficult and took longer to regain my peace. It was no fun. When I realized this pattern was affecting my ability to accomplish goals, I finally asked Heavenly Father to please help me know how to avoid these detours.

The answer came when I opened my scriptures one day. There it was—right in front of me! "Reverence thyself." Without thinking, my soul was immediately filled with the reverence I feel for the Savior and God the Father. I **felt** it and basked in it! Then, in a split second—again without thinking—a new feeling of reverence flooded my heart, except this time it was for my *Self.* I was overcome. For the first time as an adult, I experienced a deeper sense of the love God feels for each of his children than I ever had before.

Recognizing my reverence for God and the Savior, then bringing it into my heart for my *Self* was the remedy I needed! Whenever I felt inadequate, incompetent, or unworthy, I invited this same reverence into my heart, again bringing remedy. I also began Scripting these feelings to give further support.

Whether we suffer "overs" or "unders," these types of feelings arise from the *False Self*—from the ego, and from a lack of self-love, self-respect, and self-worth.

With this breakthrough, I began to understand the role the ego plays in helping us become consciously aware. By monitoring my attitude, I could feel when I started slipping into a boastful or the less-than mode, and I would immediately bring reverence back. This simple shift reined in my ego and kept it from running the show. It also kept me from continually backsliding. In fact, it helped me stay on track.

I invite you to experience reverence for your *Self*. Reverence can mean different things to different people, so you may have your own unique experience. (The standard definition is, to regard with respect and affection.)

We have reviewed how our re-actions are an outgrowth of our feelings and thoughts about our *Self* and others. We have learned how healing old emotional wounds from the past is paramount if we desire to find the peace we are seeking and re-discover our True *Self*. In the process of re-solving the past, we begin understanding our relationship with our *Self*. If we choose, this relationship can be transformed from the least fulfilling to the most fulfilling.

You have learned the importance of listening to your words, your self-talk, and your thoughts and how doing so leads to the discovery of *feelings*. Turning inward, however, is undoubtedly the most significant listening you will ever do, because the way you feel about your *Self* is basically the way you feel about others. The way you feel about your *Self* determines how you view the entire world.

The most heart-wrenching aspect of working with people is witnessing the lack of love, respect, and esteem so many have for themselves. When we view ourselves as lacking in any regard, the underlying unconscious program whispers that we can't really love ourselves. That we must first measure up—be confident, adequate, competent, worthwhile, and good enough. (Even though this was an eye-opener for me, it shouldn't have been so surprising— that's exactly how I felt most of my life! What I didn't realize was how many others felt the same way.)

Another malady that detours us is that of constantly comparing ourselves to others. This has been in affect for generations, but we continue to perpetuate it. As parents, do we say to our children, "Why aren't you more like your sister/brother/ friend?" The media contributes to comparison, as well. Sports stars, heroes, and entertainers are held up to our children to emulate. The list goes on and on— everywhere we turn! Let us claim our authenticity and individuality instead of trying to fit the mold society dictates. We can then teach our children to do the same. If we stop looking for our identity outside ourselves and go within, we will discover our own magnificent uniqueness.

> *"You were born an original. Don't die a copy."*
> —John Mason

Our uniqueness can be the most beautiful aspect of living. Continually measuring ourselves against others is as sad and irrational as the following tale.

The Animal School

Once upon a time the animals decided they must do something heroic to meet the problems of "a new world." So they organized a school.

They adopted an activity curriculum consisting of running, climbing, swimming, and flying. To make it easier to administer the curriculum, all the animals took all the subjects.

The duck was excellent in swimming, in fact better than his instructor; but he made only passing grades in flying and was very poor in running. Since he was slow in running he had to stay after school and also drop swimming in order to practice running. This was kept up until his web feet were badly worn and he was only average in swimming. But average was acceptable in school so nobody worried about that except the duck.

The rabbit started at the top of the class in running, but had a nervous breakdown because of so much make-up work in swimming.

The squirrel was excellent in climbing until he developed frustration in the flying class where his teacher made him start from the ground up instead of from the tree top down. He also developed a "charlie horse" from over-exertion, and then got a C in climbing and D in running.

The eagle was a problem child and was disciplined severely. In the climbing class he beat all the others to the top of the tree, but insisted on using his own way to get there.

At the end of the year, an abnormal eel that could swim exceedingly well, and also run, climb, and fly a little, had the highest average and was valedictorian.

—Dr. George H. Reavis

Isn't it sad that through the years our human nature has been to put everyone in slots instead of letting us be individuals and move forward at our own pace?

With all the expectations we've had placed upon us from the time we were born, is it any wonder it's a challenge to feel better about ourselves? Is it any wonder so many of us feel "less than"? When there are feelings of lack in any direction, we struggle to accomplish the seemingly impossible task of loving our *Self*. Perhaps we never achieve the goal, thereby "existing" without honestly knowing what it's like to love, reverence and honor our *Self*.

We have discussed how we acquired the origin of non-productive feelings and beliefs that keep us distanced from our *Self.* Also essential to our understanding is that we acquired some of these feelings and beliefs before we were born and at birth. As children, often we unconsciously accept what someone says about us as true, whether it is or not. We may internalize that view and allow it to contribute to our internal map. Unfortunately, our tender egos often cause us to be very vulnerable. We embrace the negative things we hear about ourselves but dismiss the positive feedback people give us. Where these feelings came from really doesn't matter. The important thing is to finally recognize the way we feel about our *Self,* take the necessary steps to re-solve the feelings that don't serve us, and continue moving toward a centered peace.

My friend, Sandra Lundberg, provided the following exchange between a customer and service rep.

Customer: I can do that. I'm not very technical, but I think I am ready to install now. What do I do first?

Rep: The first step is to open your HEART. Have you located your HEART, ma'am?

Customer: Yes I have, but there are several programs running right now. Is it okay to install while they are running?

Rep: What programs are running, ma'am?

Customer: Let me see . . . I have PASTHURT.EXE, LOWESTEEM.EXE, GRUDGE.EXE, and RESENT-MENT.COM running right now.

Rep: No problem. LOVE will automatically erase PASTHURT.EXE from your current operating system. It may remain in your permanent memory, but it will no longer disrupt other programs. LOVE will eventually overwrite LOW-ESTEEM.EXE with a module of its own called HIGH-ESTEEM.EXE. However, you have to completely turn off GRUDGE.EXE and RESENT-MENT.COM. Those programs prevent LOVE from being properly installed. Can you turn those off, ma'am?

Customer: I don't know how to turn them off. Can you tell me how?

Rep: My pleasure. Go to your Start menu and invoke FORGIVENESS.EXE. Do this as many times as necessary until GRUDGE.EXE and RESENTMENT. COM have been completely erased.

Customer: Okay, I'm done. LOVE has started installing itself automatically. Is that normal?

Rep: Yes it is. You should receive a message that says it will reinstall for the life of your HEART. Do you see that message?

Customer: Yes I do. Is it completely installed?

Rep: Yes, but remember that you have only the base program. You need to begin connecting to other HEARTS in order to get the upgrades.

Customer: Oops . . . I have an error message already. What should I do?

Rep: What does the message say?

Customer: It says ERROR 412-PROGRAM NOT RUN ON INTERNAL COMPONENTS. What does that mean?

Rep: Don't worry ma'am, that's a common problem. It means that the LOVE program is set up to run on external HEARTS but has not yet been run on your HEART. It is one of those complicated programming things, but in non-technical terms it means you have to

"LOVE" your own machine before it can "LOVE" others.

Customer: So what should I do?

Rep: Can you find the directory called SELF-ACCEPTANCE?

Customer: Yes, I have it.

Rep: Excellent, you are getting good at this.

Customer: Thank you.

Rep: You're welcome. Click on the following files and then copy them to the MYHEART Directory.

FORGIVESELF.DOC, SELFESTEEM.TXT, REA-LIZEWORTH.TXT, and GOODNESS.DOC. The system will overwrite any conflicting files and begin patching any faulty programming. Also, you need to delete SELFCRITIC.EXE from all directories, and then empty your recycle bin afterwards to make sure it is completely gone and never comes back.

Customer: Got it. Hey! My HEART is filling up with really neat files. SMILE.MPG is playing on my monitor right now and it shows that WARMTH.COM, PEACE.EXE, and CONTENTMENT.COM are copying themselves all over my HEART!

Rep: Then LOVE is installed and running. You should be able to handle it from here. One more thing before I go . . .

Customer: Yes?

Rep: LOVE is freeware. Be sure to give it and its various modules to everybody you meet. They will in turn share it with other people and they will return some really neat modules back to you.

Customer: I will. Thank you for your help.

Opening your heart is where healing begins. Moving forward is what's important. You progress rapidly when you begin accepting your life at this exact moment—realizing it just "is." Dwelling on wounds from the past or placing blame can bring you to a standstill. Rather than blaming, do your best to remember that all those who went before did the best they could. They also were products of their genetic coding, their environment, their upbringing, and their life experiences. They may have experienced abuse of every kind. Their role models may have lacked the understanding needed to raise model children.

When you consider the people around you, how often do you see someone who has a *true* sense of their own value? Feeling worthless or valueless is happening in major proportions. It's as if we have an epidemic. How tragic!

Some may disagree that we have an epidemic of people who feel worthless. Instead, they may feel too many people love themselves more than enough. I invite you to look closely at those people. Do they really love themselves, or does ego (which is there to insure survival) do a good job of projecting that image? When a person's ego is running the show, a more appropriate designation than "self-love" may be "self-absorbed" or "self-important." Is it indeed possible they act the way they do to mask feelings of inadequacy?

When someone truly loves themselves, they aren't enmeshed in their ego, or controlled by it. Neither do they find it necessary to constantly monitor their value through other's eyes. A balanced ego doesn't need regular feeding to maintain status or a place in society. They already have a stable relationship with the *Self* and with others. Those who love and possess a true sense of *Self* allow others their individuality without criticizing or trying to change them.

Some people can never receive enough adulation or reassurance from others as to their value. Their conditioning has been: *"I'm not enough."* No matter how much you commend, reassure, applaud, and express your love for them, deep inside they still feel "I'm not enough." And there is absolutely nothing you can do to change this view or fill the void their unconscious programming has created. Their modus operandi has become one of needing to top their own performance in each task they take on and in everything they do. Unconsciously, they are driven to keep working and striving so they can hopefully, someday, "be enough." They may be unaware of an internal belief that the measurement of their worth is in performance—in what they *do* instead of in who they *are*. Perhaps their subconscious programming was one of "I am only valued if I am producing something everyone can see." Or they may have been made to feel that to be noticed or admired they had to perform like a sibling, or perhaps a friend.

In my youth, it was paramount to my mother that I play the piano and sing. Every time I participated in a recital or a program, she was very pleased. Like most people who accomplish anything in music, I had to practice. I remember crying and crying because I had to practice. At the time, I didn't care about learning to play the piano! When I became belligerent, Mom just spanked me and sat me down on the piano bench. She would tell me, "I don't care how long you cry. You can cry as long as you want, but you're going to sit there until you practice an hour!" She meant it and held me to it!

My mother played the violin beautifully. I learned many years later that she would rather have played the piano. It seems she was fulfilling her desire through me. Consequently, performing was always a major part of my life. As I got older, I was very grateful to her for holding me to a practice schedule and insisting that I learn, for I have had some marvelous experiences because of my music. In fact, it was through music that I met my husband.

However, I had come to relate performing musically with acceptance. I didn't realize this until I had been married several years and was talking to a counselor who made the observation. Upon realizing my conditioning and the belief it created in me, he asked, "Did it ever occur to you that if you never played or sang another note, people might still like you?" Because I hadn't known this was my belief until that moment, it was quite a revelation. No, the thought had *never* occurred to me. Without realizing it, performing (and people's acceptance of that performance) had become my measuring stick of worth. With this startling realization, I was able to make a major shift in my life. As I let go of the old belief, I felt a sense of liberation for the first time, for I had imprisoned myself, believing that people would only like me and accept me if I performed. This was the beginning of a new lease on life.

Another unconscious, internal program these days (in sweeping proportions) is *rejection*. Hmmm . . . isn't that interesting? Might any of us have felt rejected because we were a surprise, unplanned, or unwanted pregnancy? Even if we didn't, we can still be affected by a parent's or grandparent's unresolved feelings of rejection. This happened with one of our daughters. My husband and I rejoiced greatly when we learned we were expecting her. Nevertheless, in her twenties she had to deal with feelings of rejection and the fear of being rejected—passed down from two of her grandparents.

Do you know anyone who has everything going for them (i.e. looks, talent, capabilities, intelligence, a loving spouse, beautiful children)? Yet no matter how much their friends and family love and appreciate them, they create situations that bring rejection? These people have difficulty believing others love and accept them as they are. Their internal programming (which functions from fear of rejection) unconsciously creates situations whereby they can experience rejection time after time after time. When someone feels rejected they are unable to safely accept love or build secure relationships—until the internal program at the core of their Be-ing *is* changed.

My own struggle with the legacy I established at birth ("I'm not important") and the many appendages it developed throughout the years, was very challenging to work through. Yes, I've been there and done that. So, along with other people whom I've assisted in working through their untruth, I know what a stranglehold unhealthy core feelings and beliefs can have on a person. I can't count the times I've Scripted for the appendage feelings that came with "I'm not important"– inadequate, incompetent, incapable—and similar feelings and beliefs. I knew I had to keep Scripting until I could feel the difference and know a change had taken place in the depths of my internal programming.

Finally, I began to sense change and recognize that Scripting had successfully stripped away many layers of the feelings so indelibly imbedded in me. Was the effort worth it? I will tell you this: *no* amount of money, or anything else, could persuade me to return to my former state of Be-ing!

You may be unaware of your major, unconscious, core program and wonder how to discover it. I have found the following to be some of the most apparent and recurring core programs. Note that most are fear-based:

Alone/Lost
Worthless
Need for Approval
Anger/Resentment
Guilt/Shame
Grief/Sorrow
Rejection/Abandonment
Hate/Bitterness
Not Good Enough/Not Enough
Overwhelmed
I'm a Mistake/I'm a Problem
Unaccepted/Unacceptable
Hopeless/Helpless
No Place for Me/Where Do I Belong?
Death Wish/I Don't Want to Be Here
Resignation/Martyr

Keep in mind that each core program can have numerous appendages—feelings that have spun off from the core. Layers have also compounded over the years from re-enforcing our feelings. These may also need stripping away.

How does one go about changing their unconscious internal program—their road map? Some people, after realizing what they are feeling, may have the ability to exercise

mind over matter and rid themselves of their programming without processing anything. These people are few and far between, however.

For others who would like support in making a change, Scripting can be effective in all the core programs listed. By using this tool—changing your feelings and beliefs—a major shift occurs sooner or later. Because it's unnecessary, with the Script, to recall the incidents or know the reasons for your core feelings, healing is accelerated.

Each of us is born with at least one internal core program. Some may have more. However many you have, it's all right. Whatever they are, they're part of your life's challenge, which you have the opportunity to work through. How else can we come to know our True *Self*? By taking charge of the programming we don't like, we allow our *Self* to experience a whole new lease on life.

Where does one begin? I have found that many people (subconsciously), do not **love** themselves. They neither **accept** nor **trust** themselves. Most of these people don't even **like** themselves. Interestingly enough, they all *think* they **like, love, accept,** and **trust** themselves. But they do not *feel* it.

Experience has shown that while using the Script, you can proceed much faster in all areas if you first process and resolve:

1. Feelings that keep me from liking myself;
2. Feelings that keep me from loving myself;
3. Feelings that keep me from accepting myself;
4. Feelings that keep me from trusting myself.

Therefore, the first thing I would have you do is find a comfortable, quiet place where you can sit, relax, and close your eyes. Take a deep breath through your nose and let it out slowly through your mouth. Take another deep breath the same way, only this time hold your breath at the top of the full inhalation for three counts, then let it out slowly through your mouth. This process accesses both sides of the brain. You are now ready to begin. The following is what I would say:

"Spirit/True Self (however you choose to address it), please locate the origin of the feelings that keep me from liking and loving myself. Also, locate the origin of the feelings that keep me from accepting myself and trusting myself. Take each and every level, layer, area, and aspect of my Be-ing to these origins. Analyze and resolve them perfectly with God's truth. Come forward in time, healing every incident based upon these origins, according to God's will, until I'm at the present—filled with light and truth; God's peace and love; forgiveness of myself for my incorrect perceptions; forgiveness of every person, place, circumstance, and event that has contributed to these feelings.

"With total forgiveness and unconditional love, I delete the old from my DNA, release it, and let it go *now*. I choose liking myself. I choose loving myself. I choose accepting myself exactly the way I am right now. I choose trusting myself. I like myself. I feel love for myself. I give myself permission to like and love myself. I accept myself 100%, exactly the way I am right now, knowing that until I do, I cannot move forward in my life. I feel acceptance of myself. I am my own best friend. I feel trust in myself that with the help of God, I can accomplish my goals. I give myself permission to succeed in all my endeavors!"

Then finish the rest of the Script (in the Introduction).

Recently I received a phone call from Ann. She shared that upon realizing she didn't like, love, accept, or trust herself, she Scripted for these feelings. Her desire was to be aligned with the four feelings daily, until they became a natural part of her. Ann shared her method of keeping these feelings on the tip of her tongue. She simply rearranged them so that she could more consistently stand TALL— Trusting, Accepting, Liking and Loving herself. As a reminder and a trigger to herself, she would simply say, "Stand TALL, Ann. Stand TALL"—meaning, I Trust myself, I Accept myself, I Like myself, and I Love myself.

While you are learning to embrace self-trust, self-acceptance, self-like, and self-love, may I suggest you add self-respect and self-validation. You may be going through life without respecting your *Self*, or without feeling validated as a worthwhile human Be-ing. (This is what happened to me. I just discovered a few years ago that I didn't feel validated.) Script for the feelings that keep you from respecting and validating your *Self*. ("Spirit, please locate the origin of my feelings that keep me from respecting myself and validating myself.")

If others have a difficult time trusting, accepting, liking, loving, respecting, or validating us, it's usually due to our inability to feel these things for our *Self*. And because we unwittingly put out one or more of these messages, we experience the "echo" effect.

Without realizing it, we draw people into our relationships and our life who support how we feel about our *Self*. After this happens enough times, we begin to wonder why others don't accept, love, or validate us. Eventually, we may see what we have unconsciously been doing to our *Self*.

Changing the perception of your *Self* and feeling better about who you are and what you are may take consistent effort. Regardless, the effort is worth while! Pray to God that He will assist you in Be-ing able to love your *Self* the way He does—that you will be able to see your *Self* through His eyes. Your ultimate objective is to unconditionally love and reverence your *Self* as the unique Be-ing that you are.

Your finest occupation is *Be-ing*. By Be-ing your *Self*, peace will find a place in your heart and you will feel better in every facet of your life. Achieving the energy shift you would like—within your own boundaries, within your True *Self*—is worth any and all the effort required.

How important is it that we love our *Self*? Can we give something to someone else if we don't have it ourselves? It is impossible to truly love others if we don't first love our *Self*.

One Morning's Prayer

I go out every morning, the sun's not risen yet.
I gaze up at the stars, a sight I'll ne'er forget.
My heart is filled with wonder of the blessings that are mine,
And I pause to ponder . . . on things that are Divine.

In need of reassurance, I offered up this prayer,
"Do you really love me, do you really care?"
"Silly you, Of course I do," so gentle His reply,
Overwhelmed by His pure Love, I began to cry.

"There's more I need to tell you, there's more for you to hear."
It's like His arms went 'round me so he could
whisper in my ear.
"See yourself as I see you, my precious little one,
Love yourself as I love you, that's how it must be done."

"The first and great commandment is to Love Me
with all your heart.
The second like unto it, can't be done without this part.
To love thy neighbor as thyself, first starts with loving you.
Without which thy neighbor's slighted . . .
believe Me, this is true.
Doing it unto the least of these is doing it unto Me.
Loving yourself is loving Me too, so now I'm sure you see,
Being the best and doing the most that
I need you to do,
Can't be done unless you learn, that
you must love you, too!"

—Ruth C. Price

CHAPTER 20

What Is the Purpose?

The mind has no power to change your life.
That privilege belongs to the heart alone.

—Glenda Green

Why are we even reading this book? Why are we interested in *re-searching* ourselves to the point of getting to know who we are? What is the purpose of our seeking? Is there another way of coming to know who we are, other than *re-searching* our feelings?

Several years ago, one of my brothers gave me the book, The *Dragon Doesn't Live Here Anymore,* by Alan Cohen. I love the title. To me it means the inner conflict doesn't live here—inside—anymore.

Facing your dragons—those less than glorious feelings, those unbridled emotions that drive you and create your inner conflicts—takes courage. But you don't have to do it alone. Although most of us cannot see it because it is in the subtle energy field, all kinds of assistance are available to us from the Heavenly realms. In breaking free from the claws of the dragon, we would be wise to ask daily for Divine direction, Divine wisdom, and Divine assistance in obtaining our freedom.

I know there are many people who are willing to re-solve, or have already begun re-solving, their inner conflicts. Oh, that we could hear all their stories. I congratulate and commend them for their desire to create a difference in their lives and subsequently, in the lives of others. With enough people re-solving their inner conflicts, eventually the shifting energies will become apparent and major transformations will take place. In fact, I believe they are already in progress.

How would life be if the majority of us were willing to look inside and become absolutely congruent in our feelings, thoughts, words, and actions—coming from love? How refreshing the outcome if each of us took off our mask and spoke our truth—with pure intent—from our heart! Who was it that showed us the way by His example?

In January of 1999, I received a most unusual letter from a woman who had read *Feelings Buried Alive Never Die* . . . and decided to put the Script to the test. What she shared with me spoke volumes. I offer this woman's experience for however it may benefit you.

In April, just before Easter, my husband, my 17 year old daughter and I visited a bigger-than-life sized statue of the Christus. We discussed the Atonement of the Savior. We talked about His bleeding from every pore, His life and what Easter was really about. As we drove home, the discussion continued in the car.

When we arrived home, I again continued to read your book. I wasn't really convinced about the *Script* and was even a little doubtful that the *Script* could make a difference. I did

believe in the power of prayer for I have experienced many answers to prayer, and it was prayer that had kept me going each day. Because the *Script* seemed to be like a prayer to me, I decided I would try it.

I thought about one feeling that I felt was a major problem in my life. I came to the conclusion that guilt was a major feeling for me because I accepted guilt for all my children's actions, and guilt for things that went wrong in my day-to-day life. My father had actually disciplined by creating guilt feelings when I was a child. As a consequence, I never wanted to do anything to disappoint my parents. So guilt was the feeling I decided to first process through the *Script*.

As I began to process guilt through the *Script* and replace it with forgiveness of myself—so that I could receive peace of mind and feel love in my life—chills began in my brain and continued throughout my whole body. And then on my right arm just above the wrist area, one pore began to bleed. This pore bled to the point that it bled on my book. I was so amazed at what was happening to me that I walked into the family room and showed my husband what was happening. I looked at my arm to see if there was a sore or some reason for it to be bleeding. There was not. The next day, I still looked at my arm for a sore, scabs, etc., for an explanation of why the pore began bleeding. There was no sign of an injury. My arm was normal. I can still look at my arm and see the pore that bled that night, and the most amazing thing is that I feel so different. I do not feel guilty for anyone's problems anymore. I am completely over the guilt within my soul. I had feelings of anger towards my father for some childhood disciplinary actions that I felt had been really unfair—but it really doesn't matter anymore.

I have shared my book with many others and have given the book as gifts. One neighbor was having some problems with a child, and she has been helped so much that she shared the book with her friends. But I always make sure I get my book back, as the blood on page 176 and 177 reminds me of the power within our Souls, and that God can and does heal if we know how to unite our physical body with our spiritual body and become one in unity.

Thank you for the information you have put together within this book that has changed my life. The experience I had with the *Script* has testified to me about the real meaning of the atonement of Jesus Christ. We *can* have forgiveness and healing for our incorrect feelings that we create within ourselves.

Sincerely, Lou Ann Pecorelli

Is the Lord there for you? Is it possible to know Him without knowing your *Self*? What is the benefit of coming to know your True *Self* and claiming your Divine inheritance? Could it all have to do with your purpose for being here? Is it your purpose, by any chance, to re-claim the *Love*—to *Be* the *Love* that you already are? Would this raise your vibrational frequencies to more ably resonate with the man who came here to show the way? How can you *Be* this Love or *Be* like Him as long as you are weighed down with inner conflicts and negativity—if you are at odds with members of your family—with your fellow man?

If cleansing the inner vessel is in progress, vibrational frequencies *are* being elevated. Can enough of us "cleanse the inner vessel" to have an impact? Might this in part help curtail such historical events as Columbine High School? Can you make a difference?

It may all sound too complicated or too difficult, but it really isn't. All it takes is caring and commitment. Dr.

Carolyn Myss strongly suggests that we, "Release our dead!" Holding onto the past interferes with what the Divine is striving to do in our present. Resurrect your *Self*— your True *Self*. Come back to life—real life! (It has been said that many of us die years before we are buried.)

And how do you come back to your real life?

Let us review the eight R's:

1) Recognize your negative energies (words, self-talk, thoughts, feelings, actions and behaviors), and change them to positive energies.

2) Recognize your "inner enemy," acknowledge him/her as your own, and find his/her constructive side. Learn what is necessary to learn from him/her.

3) Recognize the futility of blame and judgment and re-move it from your life.

4) Recognize the role ego and pride play in your life.

5) Realize that making mistakes are part of life's lessons.

6) Recognize the importance of Love in all aspects of your existence, and embrace the intrinsic Love in everyone—including your Self.

7) Remove the wall keeping you from the Love that you are.

8) Resolve to re-store your true, inherent, Divine nature, the Love that you are.

The tools in this book for accomplishing the eight R's are:

1) Scripting

2) Vocalizing

3) Revising

4) Writing Forgivenesses

5) Silent Processing of Spirit to Spirit/Heart to Heart/Mind to Mind

With all of these processes please remember Prayer. Begin and end each process with your supplication to God. When you pray, along with bringing God into your healing, you center your Be-ing.

Let's say that you are successful in leveling the wall you have built. Here you are—standing at your door. While standing there, if you go within your *Self*, you will notice that you feel differently from how you felt when you started on this journey. You will also notice that your door—the door that allows entrance to your True *Self*—has no door knob. But, if you come to this door in truth

Letting go of separateness—recognizing and
appreciating your individuality;
Better understanding and knowing your Self
WITH your heart—FROM your heart;
Unconditionally accepting your Self and others
WITH your heart—FROM your heart;
Trusting God WITH all your heart—
FROM your heart;
Totally forgiving everyone, WITH your heart—
FROM your heart;
Allowing each person their own experiences without
it changing the nature of who you are;
Extending mercy to everyone WITH your heart—

FROM your heart;
LOVING all God's children, including your Self,
WITH your heart—FROM your heart;
Feeling boundless gratitude WITH your heart—
FROM your heart;
Feeling compassion WITH all your heart—
FROM your heart;
And Be-ing the Love that you are WITH your heart—
FROM your heart;

then, your door may already be open. And if, per chance, there is still more cleansing to do, you can continue doing it and ultimately realize your goal of coming to know the Love that you are.

May God assist you in opening this most meaningful door and experiencing the wonder and joy of re-uniting with the Truth of your Be-ing; may you bask in the re-sounding thrill of re-storing the Love that you are and re-claiming your "heart of gold." May the experience of *Healing Feelings . . . From Your Heart* bring you to know the Lord of Lords—King of Kings, and be the most meaningful emotional and spiritual accomplishment you ever achieve. And may the resulting freedom of this re-union be yours, from that moment on. . . .

About the Cover Artist

Valerieann J. Skinner grew up in a small town in southeastern Idaho. In this environment she was not exposed to the traditional do's and don'ts of art, which allowed her to develop her own unique way of expression through her paintings. Valerieann has won many awards for her work over the years, especially for her beautiful, realistic portrayals of wildlife and horses. Although she became expert at painting in a more traditional style early in her career, she found herself yearning to move into a deeper expression of herself. Her innate desire was to be able to paint from her heart and to express herself on canvas without barriers or limitations.

It wasn't until she began exploring her feelings and painting from "within" that her art took a dramatic turn and became truly transcendent. This change transpired during her journey of self-discovery as she began utilizing the Script and the principles presented in *Feelings Buried Alive Never Die . . .* , and working with the author in digging a little deeper to find her True-Self.

As a result, Valerieann explains, "I began a journey with my painting that awakened in me the ability to freely express visions, feelings, and knowing beyond the physical. I have also been able to teach others how to do the same. The joy experienced while creating in this way and sharing it with others is exquisite!"

Valerieann relies on a deep, abiding spirituality to guide her work—creating after periods of repose, meditation, and communion with her Maker. Viewers of her art feel this spiritual element as an inner sense of peace and calm. By combining her realistic techniques and her more inward approach, she has been able to infuse her paintings with greater depth and feeling.

In 1995 Valerieann painted the cover of the second edition of *Feelings Buried Alive Never Die . . .* , and in 1999, the cover of this book, *Healing Feelings . . . From Your Heart*. Both covers are truly inspired and invoke the exact feelings the author desired. For this and the design of the cover and book, the author is most grateful.

For art prints or greeting cards of the original cover painting, or for learning the importance of colors and how they impact your life, contact:
Valerieann J. Skinner
Phone 208-847-3129
vskinner@directinter.net
www.valerieann.com

Copyright Acknowledgments

For permission to use copyrighted material the author gratefully acknowledges the following:

There are many quotes included herein for which we were unable to acquire the author or the source. We would indeed like to give the appropriate persons acknowledgment for these. If any of you have access to this information, we would truly appreciate learning about it so that appropriate acknowledgment can be made in further editions.

Suggested Reading

Allen, Charles L., *God's Psychiatry*, Jove Publications, Inc., New York, New York 10016, 1978

Arterburn, Stephen, *Hand-Me-Down Genes & Second-Hand Emotions*, Fireside (Simon & Schuster), New York, New York 10020, 1994

Bloodworth, Venice, *Key to Yourself*, DeVorss & Company, Marina del Rey, California 90294, 1980

Brinkley, Dannion, *At Peace in the Light*, Harper Collins Publishers, Inc., New York, New York 10022, 1995

Carroll, Lee & Jan Tober, *The Indigo Children*, Hay House, Inc., Carlsbad, California 92018-5100, 1999

Cohen, Alan, *The Dragon Doesn't Live Here Anymore*, Alan Cohen Publications & Workshops, Somerset, New Jersey 08875, 1981

Covey, Stephen R., *The Divine Center*, Bookcraft, Salt Lake City, Utah, 1982

Covey, Stephen R., *Seven Habits of Highly Successful People*, Simon & Schuster, Rockefeller Center, 1230 Avenue of the Americas, N.Y., N.Y. 10020

Dyer, Wayne, *The Secrets to Manifesting Your Destiny*, Nightingale-Conant Corp., Niles, Illinois 60714

Eadie, Betty J., *Embraced by the Light*, and *The Ripple Effect*, c/o Onjinjinkta, Seattle WA 98125, 1999

Eyre, Linda & Richard, *Teaching Your Children Sensitivity*, A Fireside Book (Simon & Schuster) New York, New York 10020, 1995

Glasser, Howard, and Jennifer Easley, *Transforming the Difficult Child*, Center for Difficult Child Publications

Green, Glenda, *Love Without End*, Heartwings Publishing, Fort Worth, Texas 76117, 1999

Goleman, Daniel, *Emotional Intelligence*, Bantam Books, New York, New York 10036, 1995

Jampolsky, Gerald G., M.D. and L. Lee, Ph.D., *Listen To Me . . .*, Celestial Arts, Berkeley, California 94707, 1996

Joslyn, Joy Tsuya & Don, *The First Note*, Art Farm Productions, Coloma, California 95613, 1995

Latham, Dr. Glenn I., *Christlike Parenting*, Gold Leaf Press, 415 Neal Armstrong Rd., Salt Lake City, Utah 84116, 2000

Lundberg, Gary B. & Joy Saunders, *I Don't Have to Make Everything All Better*, Viking Penguin Press, Hudson, New York, 10014-3657, 1995

Mills, Roy, *The Soul's Rembrance*, Onjinjinkta Publishing, Seattle, WA 98125, 1999

Skinner, Valerieann J., *Courage to Live Your Truth*, 2001. e-Book found on www.valerieann.com

Truman, Karol K., *Feelings Buried Alive Never Die . . .* , Olympus Distributing, Las Vegas, Nevada, 89193-7693, 1995

Two Listeners, (Edited by A. J. Russell) *God Calling*, Jove Book, New York, New York 10016, 1978

Robbins, Anthony, *Awaken the Giant Within*, A Fireside Book, Simon & Schuster, New York, New York, 10020, 1992

Dear Reader,

Take advantage of my free questionnaire to discover which negative feelings you need to begin resolving. You will find it at www.healingfeelings.com.

While you are there you can also learn about 100% pure therapeutic Essential Oils–their unique frequencies and how they can bless your life.

If you do not have access to the internet, call 1-800-531-3180 for more information.

If you are interested in a tape of Brent's music, mentioned in Chapter 12, call 1-800-531-3180.

God bless you in your efforts.

Karol K. Truman